MEDICINE ON THE BATTLEFIELD

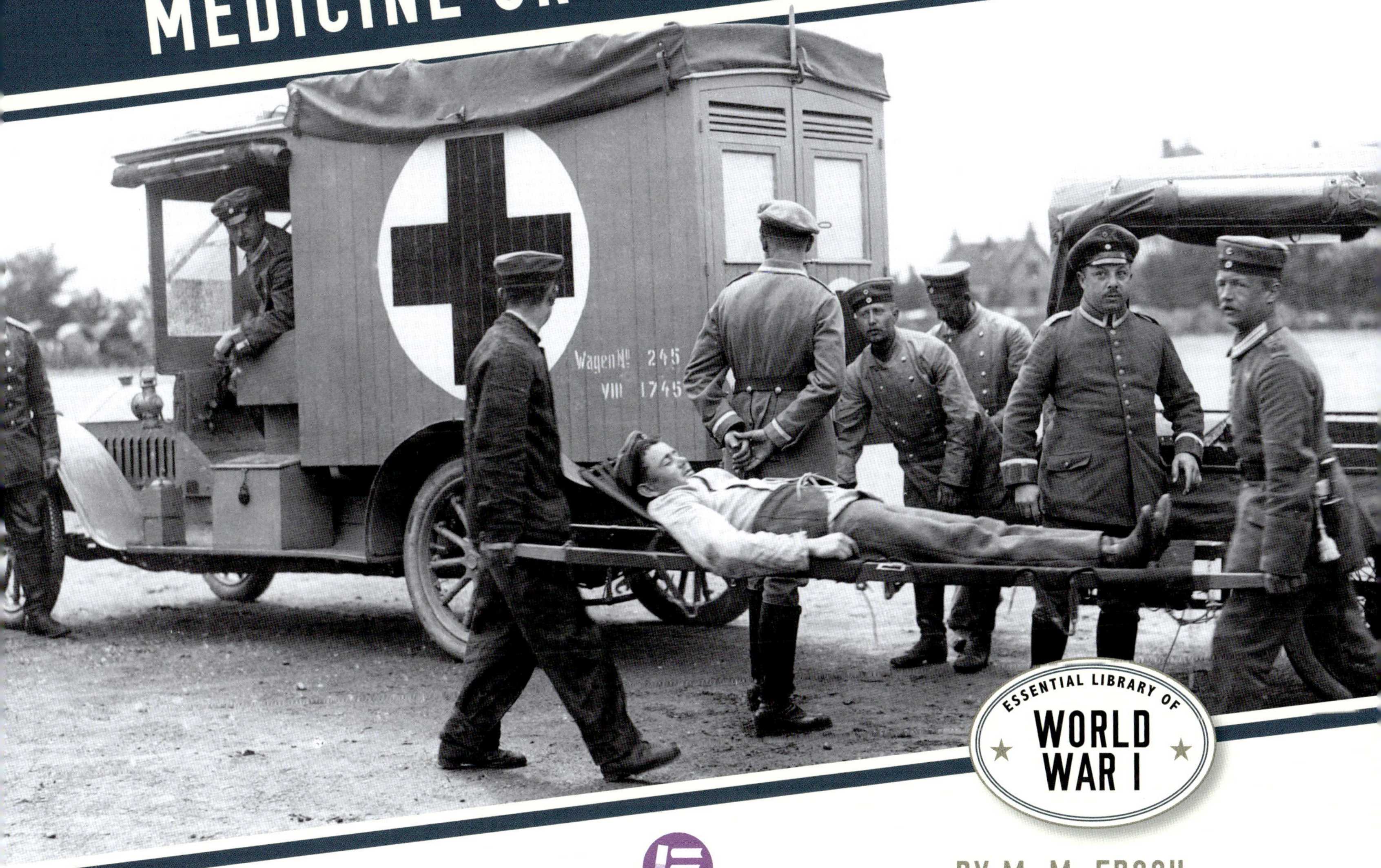

ESSENTIAL LIBRARY OF WORLD WAR I

BY M. M. EBOCH

CONTENT CONSULTANT

HEATHER R. PERRY, PHD
ASSOCIATE PROFESSOR OF HISTORY
UNIVERSITY OF NORTH CAROLINA AT CHARLOTTE

Essential Library

An Imprint of Abdo Publishing
abdopublishing.com

abdopublishing.com

Published by Abdo Publishing, a division of ABDO, PO Box 398166, Minneapolis, Minnesota 55439.

Printed in the United States of America, North Mankato, Minnesota

092015
012016

THIS BOOK CONTAINS
RECYCLED MATERIALS

Cover Photo: Berliner Verlag/Archiv/Picture-Alliance/DPA/AP Images
Interior Photos: Berliner Verlag/Archiv/Picture-Alliance/DPA/AP Images, 1, 91; Library of Congress, 4; Imperial War Museum (Q 81810), 7; Susan Law Cain/Shutterstock Images, 9; Everett Historical/Shutterstock Images, 11, 14, 27, 48, 62, 72, 96, 99 (top), 99 (bottom); The Print Collector/Heritage Images/Glow Images, 19, 21, 25; Lady Francis Balfour CC4.0, 29; Lawrence Wilbur/Library of Congress, 33; akg-images/Newscom, 34; Oxford Science Archive/Heritage Images/Glow Images, 39, 98; Bain News Service/Library of Congress, 42, 51; Paul Thompson/National Geographic Creative/Corbis, 46; National Geographic Creative/Corbis, 52; Harris & Ewing Collection/Library of Congress, 54; Archiv Neumann/Picture-Alliance/DPA/AP Images, 56, 67; Underwood & Underwood/Corbis, 59; Hulton-Deutsch Collection/Corbis, 64; Otis Historical Archives National Museum of Health and Medicine, 68, 83; Thomas Keith Aitken/Imperial War Museum (Q 11586), 76; Handout/MCT/Newscom, 78; United Kingdom Government, 80; Everett Collection/Newscom, 86; Stefan Sauer/Picture Alliance/ZB/Newscom, 88; AP Images, 95

Editor: Jenna Gleisner
Series Designers: Kelsey Oseid and Maggie Villaume

Library of Congress Control Number: 2015945639

Cataloging-in-Publication Data

Eboch, M. M.
Medicine on the battlefield / M. M. Eboch.
p. cm. -- (Essential library of World War I)
ISBN 978-1-62403-923-2 (lib. bdg.)
Includes bibliographical references and index.
1. World War, 1914-1918--Medical care--Juvenile literature. 2. Medicine, military--United States--History--20th century--Juvenile literature. I. Title.
940.4--dc23

2015945639

CONTENTS

Medical personnel, such as this Red Cross nurse in Antwerp, Belgium, learned as they went, forced to treat more soldiers than most hospitals could handle.

CHAPTER 1

IN THE MIDST OF BATTLE

The medical staff had arrived in Veurne, Belgium, only the day before. They started cleaning the filthy building, an old college. It would be their hospital for the winter of 1914. But it was dark and poorly equipped, with only a few beds. Even worse, many of their hospital supplies had disappeared, perhaps stolen during their travels.

When an ambulance arrived, Henry Souttar, the physician in charge, hurried to greet the medical workers. The ambulance held two badly wounded officers, and the driver asked whether the hospital was ready to receive patients. Souttar had replied they were not. How could they treat injuries when they had no supplies?

The ambulance attendants said the only other option was to send the wounded to France. They might reach help in two or three days. The hospital took in the men. Another ambulance arrived an hour later, and within four days they had 350 patients.

THE WORLD AT WAR

Souttar, a surgeon at London Hospital, had volunteered when the war, which would become known as World War I, broke out in 1914. The war had seemed to explode out of almost nothing. A small group of Serbs wanted freedom from the empire controlled by Austria-Hungary. Gavrilo Princip, a member of the group, killed Austria-Hungary's Archduke Franz Ferdinand and his wife during a parade in Sarajevo, Bosnia, on June 28, 1914. Austria then made demands of Serbia, some of which Serbia refused to meet. On July 28, 1914, Austria attacked. While troops mobilized, diplomats throughout Europe tried to prevent a full-blown war. Yet no one was willing to back down, and countries not directly involved felt obligated to support their allies. The United Kingdom, France, and Russia made up the Allies, or the Triple Entente. Austria-Hungary, Germany, and the Ottoman Empire made up the Central powers. Later, Japan, Italy, and other countries joined the Allied forces. The United States would not join the Allies until 1917.

Young men on both sides signed up for war joyfully, expecting victory and honor within a few months at most. Yet the war dragged out for four years with unprecedented destruction. New weapons were introduced, including larger, more deadly artillery, tanks, machine guns, flamethrowers, and poison gas. Submarines brought the battle underwater, while aircraft attacked from the sky.

The new machine guns could fire up to 600 rounds per minute. They splintered bones and tore flesh. Compared to earlier guns, machine guns wounded more people quickly and also caused multiple wounds in one person. A victim might have injuries in the head, chest, abdomen, and several limbs. Machine guns could also overheat and explode, injuring the people operating them. Explosive weapons

The assassination of Franz Ferdinand, *center*, and his wife, Sophie, sparked the events leading to World War I.

caused similar damage from flying shrapnel. To make matters worse, wounds easily became infected because of the muddy, filthy trenches soldiers lived in, and even a slight injury and infection could be deadly.

An estimated 10 million soldiers were killed in World War I, with another 20 million crippled or badly wounded.[1] More than one-half of the troops who fought in the war were dead, wounded, or missing by the time the war ended.[2] Civilians also perished from bombs and shells or from the hunger and disease spread by wartime conditions.

NEW WEAPONS OF WAR

The number of World War I casualties was so high in large part because of newer, more lethal weapons. Artillery and mortars could fire farther and faster, and artillery killed more people than any other weapon could. Machine guns could mow down approaching troops. Handheld flamethrowers sprayed fuel oil that was ignited as it left the device. Poison gases killed few but incapacitated many and caused extensive pain and terror. Airplanes, a relatively new invention, were first used to find information about the enemy. Later they were armed with machine guns and then bombs. Submarines could attack with torpedoes underwater or could surface to use guns on deck. With these new weapons, death came from every direction.

DO OR DIE

When Souttar joined the British forces, he was appointed surgeon in chief of the Belgian field hospitals. The British and French were fighting in Belgium to protect the country against Germany and to prevent Germany from moving onward into France. In Antwerp, Belgium, Souttar set up a hospital for casualties from the Belgian army. The hospital was large, with 150 beds and excellent equipment. A staff

US soldiers learn to use machine guns at Camp Sherman in Chillicothe, Ohio, preparing them for war.

of approximately 50 included eight doctors, 20 nurses, and various assistants. The wards were already full when Souttar arrived, with some serious cases, but he noted the wounded were cheerful.

The battlefront, where opposing forces met and clashed, was many miles away, and the hospital staff expected the battle to keep its distance. In previous wars, serious injuries had generally been treated in hospitals far back from the front lines. Yet the German army quickly pushed forward toward Antwerp, and the hospital wards filled with wounded soldiers. Then the Germans started bombing Antwerp itself. As the city emptied, the hospital staff moved all patients to the basement for safety. After a shell landed in the garden, orders came to evacuate. London double-decker buses, converted for war use, collected the medical staff and patients. The staff, all patients, and much of the equipment was safely shuttled away.

Souttar's team did not have much of a break before they were sent again to

A WORLD OF CHALLENGES

World War I eventually involved more than 30 countries from throughout Europe, North Africa, the Middle East, and Asia. Medical personnel had to adapt to the special challenges of where they were stationed, whether jungle, swamp, or the heat and sand of a desert. They might face rain and mud or snow and bitter cold. They might be stationed on land or at sea. Each climate brought new challenges in terms of the local diseases and terrain.

In a war that took place over an extensive area, specific injuries and illnesses varied from place to place. Doctors in France and Russia primarily had to treat wounded soldiers. Sickness abounded in the Balkans and East Africa. The Serbian armies' death rate reached 40 percent because of the disease typhus and other epidemics in the Balkans.[3]

German troops occupy Antwerp in 1915.

the front lines, this time in Veurne. They set up a hospital approximately five miles (8 km) from the front. Before they could get beds and supplies, their help was needed. "The cases we had seen at Antwerp were nothing to these," Souttar recalled. "Arms and legs were torn right off or hanging by the merest shreds, ghastly wounds of the head left the brain exposed. Many of the poor fellows were taken from the ambulances dead, and of the others at least half must have died." The hospital staff worked day and night with poor equipment, even trying to amputate legs with a saw designed for fingers. "There was nothing else for it," Souttar noted. "Either the work had to be done or the patients had to die. And there was certainly no one else to do it."[4]

RETURN TO ACTION

A primary goal of wartime medical service was to get wounded men back into the fighting. This was not a medical decision, but a military one. An army that ran out of soldiers would fail. Millions of soldiers died during combat or from diseases. Tens of millions were wounded. Sick and wounded soldiers often had to return to battle as soon as possible, even if they were not fully recovered. Doctors might have to release patients much sooner than they wanted. More than one-half of the soldiers admitted to British hospitals at the western front were sent from the hospital back to the fighting.[5]

NEVER LOSE HOPE

Members of the medical staff learned as they worked. The nurses developed a system for bringing the nearly dead back to life. They cleaned mud off the patient and laid him down with bags of hot water packed around him. A warm saline solution, administered intravenously, helped warm chilled bodies and fight dehydration. When the patient could raise his head, he was given hot coffee with brandy, as well as morphine for the pain. These simple treatments helped many patients recover to a remarkable degree.

For all the medical staff, the work was often discouraging and horrifying, as well as exhausting, hard physical labor. Still, Souttar said, "We soon learnt to give up no case as hopeless."[6] Without doctors such as Souttar, and all the medical staff who worked with him, the shocking death toll of the war would have been even higher.

World War I marked the first extensive use of organized trench warfare.

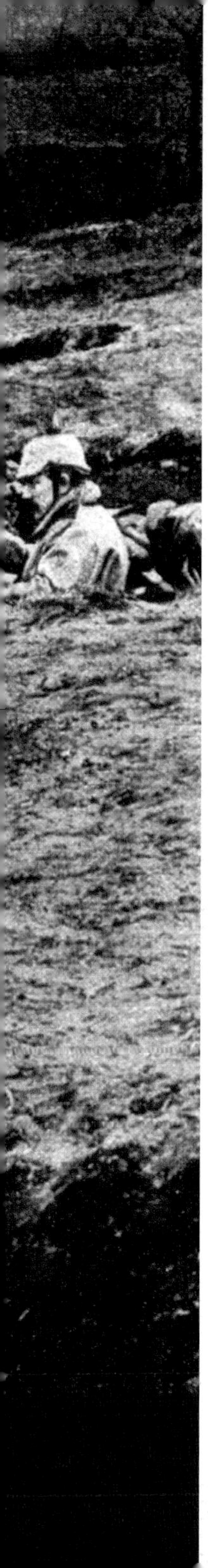

CHAPTER 2

GETTING HELP FAST

The western front extended approximately 500 miles (800 km) through Belgium and France. There, the Germans fought the French and Belgian armies, which were aided by the United Kingdom, Australia, Canada, Russia, and eventually the United States. The United Kingdom and France ruled colonies in Africa, India, and Southeast Asia. Local troops were drawn from these countries to fight in Europe too. At the start of the war, one of every three soldiers under British command in France was from India.[1]

At the western front, battles were largely fought from trenches, which offered soldiers some protection from attack. Each side dug more than 12,000 miles (19,300 km) of trenches during the war. The Germans built complex tunnel and trench structures. Some had living quarters 50 feet (15 m) below ground, with electricity, beds, and toilets.

The Allies dug trenches approximately 6 feet (2 m) deep and 2 feet (0.6 m) wide at the bottom. They were open to the air or perhaps covered with canvas. They made a frontline trench from 50 yards (46 m) to one mile (1.6 km) away from the German's front trench. A few hundred yards behind that, a support trench held men and supplies ready to assist the frontline trench. Several hundred yards farther back, a reserve trench held more men and supplies. They stayed ready for emergencies if the front trenches were taken by the enemy. Communication trenches connected the other trenches, allowing the movement of people, messages, and supplies.

In between the Allied and German trenches was no-man's-land, an area filled with artillery craters and barbed wire. At night, men crawled into no-man's-land to eavesdrop on the enemy or conduct raids. Many soldiers died trying to advance into no-man's-land.

Initially, wounded soldiers were removed from the trenches and taken to hospitals for treatment. After the first major battle, several problems became clear. First, medical help could not be located far from the battle. The wounded often died before reaching help. Additional ambulances were rushed to the front, putting medical personnel right in the line of fire along with soldiers. Hospitals also had to move closer to the battlefields. Field hospitals were set up in abandoned buildings or in tents, often close enough to the fighting to hear the battle. This system of field hospitals is still used in wartime.

SORTING THE WOUNDED

Medical services needed a way to sort the patients. The concept of triage, or the decision of which patient should be treated first, was simple: treat the wounded according to the severity of their injuries. Those with minor injuries could wait, whereas serious injuries were handled immediately. Anyone mortally wounded could be helped only by easing their suffering. The idea of triage was radical when it was first introduced in the 1790s. Before that, the wounded were treated based on their rank or class, with upper-class officers receiving help first.

THE GOLDEN HOUR

In World War I, the French gathered data to support the theory that seriously injured patients have a better chance of survival if they are treated quickly. They found that patients treated within one hour had a 10 percent mortality rate. That death rate climbed to 75 percent for patients who did not receive care for ten hours or more. This goal of treating serious wounds within one hour later became known as the "golden hour."[2]

Belgian surgeon Antoine Depage introduced a five-step triage system early in World War I. Depage had experienced some of the challenges of wartime medicine while establishing hospitals during the Balkans War (1912–1913) shortly before World War I. His triage steps covered both the transportation and the treatment of wounded patients.

The British army's Royal Army Medical Corps set up a system for medical care. The wounded were first treated at the collecting zone, closest to the battlefield. Soldiers often fought from the protection of trenches, so the collecting zone could be part of the trench system. There, the regimental medical officer (MO) did initial treatment. The MO cleaned and bandaged wounds, splinted broken limbs, and tried to keep the soldier warm to prevent shock. In medical terms, shock happens when the body does not provide enough blood flow to the organs. It is a life-threatening condition that must be treated quickly. Soldiers with minor wounds were quickly treated and sent back into combat.

In some places the battle lines moved more often, so soldiers did not usually fight from trenches. This happened at the western front at the start and toward the end of the war. This meant sick and wounded soldiers had to be transported farther and more frequently. Sometimes transportation was impossible, so wounded soldiers were left behind. The enemy took the lucky ones prisoner and provided medical treatment.

RISKING LIVES TO SAVE LIVES

Although trench warfare meant fairly permanent aid stations could be set up close to front lines, it created a challenge because the field of battle was rarely abandoned. In earlier conflicts, doctors might wait until the battle had ended before going out to treat the wounded. In World War I, battles were fought across

If a wound immobilized a soldier, the MO or other help might work in the frontline trenches.

a few hundred feet of ground, leaving hundreds of wounded between the two sides' trenches. In theory, Red Cross workers should have been able to aid the wounded safely, under the protection of their medical symbol. However, the Red Cross symbol was often not respected during World War I. Medical personnel were targeted just as much as the soldiers.

Once a soldier was wounded, help might not come for hours as the battle raged on. During heavy fighting, wounded soldiers might have to lie in the trenches until dark made it safer for stretcher bearers to reach them. To make matters worse, many soldiers were in poor condition even before they were wounded. They had lived in the trenches for weeks, damp and dirty, exposed to harsh weather. Soldiers in the trenches rarely got enough sleep or healthy food. They were often in very bad shape by the time medical help arrived.

ROUNDING CORNERS

Transporting injured soldiers to safety was challenging. Stretcher bearers had to retrieve the injured from the field of battle, sometimes in the midst of fighting. When possible, they traveled in the trenches, but trenches were narrow and made a zigzag pattern to prevent attacks from the sides. Trenches were also filled with fighting soldiers and other obstacles. A rigid wooden stretcher was difficult to maneuver. A flexible stretcher, made in Britain starting in 1915, made it easier to navigate corners and get the wounded to help quickly. The stretcher had a canvas hammock suspended from a jointed pole.

Stretcher bearers often worked in the thick of fighting, and many of them were killed.

WOMEN OF ALL WORK

A shortage of doctors meant nurses sometimes did tasks they would not have been allowed to do at home. This included making decisions about triage patients, administering morphine, and sometimes offering more advanced first aid. Australian nurse Madeline Wilson wrote in her diary that she "had to plug one bullet wound in back, with finger till doctor could come, all Doctors busy with non stop operations, one after the other, this soldier lived."[5]

THE FIRST RESPONDERS

Stretcher bearers were usually the first to treat the wounded. In ideal circumstances, if the fighting had stopped and the terrain was easy, four bearers could bring a wounded man to the first aid post within an hour. In reality, it often took eight men to carry a laden stretcher through heavy rain and mud.

Stretcher bearers worked at the hospitals as well, serving the function of orderlies. They carried patients between the wards and the operating rooms. They cleaned wards, scrubbed the floors, burned the soiled dressings, and cleaned the stretchers, which Souttar called "a very difficult and unpleasant job."[3]

The stretcher bearers at Souttar's hospital were Belgians, mostly educated men, such as teachers, who could not serve in the army for some reason. "They were quite ready to do any work we might require at any hour of the day or night," Souttar said.[4] Other British orderlies were often English or Indian soldiers who had minimal medical training. Nurses had to train and direct the orderlies in the midst of chaos. To make matters worse, there was high turnover, as orderlies were often sent to replace dead or wounded field ambulance staff.

SPEEDY RESCUERS

Once the wounded were away from the battle, ambulance drivers transported them between aid stations. At the beginning of the war, ambulances were carts drawn by horses. These had some advantage compared with motorized vehicles on muddy, uneven ground. However, they could not handle the large number of wounded. Motorized ambulances were quickly added, although horse-drawn ambulances still had some use throughout the war. Ambulances often worked under the cover of darkness and could not use lights. A team member might walk the road in front of the ambulance, leading it around potholes.

Sometimes ambulance speed determined whether a patient lived or died. Ambulances drove on rough roads that had been badly damaged by fighting and sometimes found themselves in the midst of battle. An ambulance could take the wounded soldier to a dressing station, where first aid was provided.

STEP BY STEP

Less serious wounds were dressed and sent on to hospitals for additional treatment. Emergency cases were treated immediately. Those with mortal wounds were given morphine or chloroform to ease the pain. In times of heavy fighting, even patients with severe but treatable wounds might be left to die. In military terms, it was more important to get slightly wounded soldiers back to battle.

Although there were some differences between countries, most armies had a similar system. Injured soldiers received emergency first aid at the front, and dressing stations did more work close by. Field hospitals or casualty clearing stations (CCSs) a few miles away housed patients who needed more extensive care. Some wounded were transferred even farther back to base hospitals where they could receive long-term care. The most extensive medical services were the farthest away from the front.

HOSPITAL TRAINS

Whereas many injured soldiers received care close to the front lines, those with serious injuries requiring extensive treatment were sent to distant hospitals. For the Allies fighting in Belgium, this meant a long train trip to Calais, France. The journey often took a day or longer. Souttar noted, "It is not good treatment, but good surgery is not the primary object of war. The fighting troops are the first consideration, and the surgeon has to manage the best way he can."[6] Germany had approximately 150 hospital trains, which had operating suites for conducting surgery.

Some were operated by the military and generally did not allow female nurses onboard. Early in the war, wounded Russian soldiers suffered from terrible conditions on hospital trains, with no nursing care. Hospital trains improved during the war, supported by Russian nobility.

Most medical personnel believed in the war effort. That did not mean they agreed with every decision officials made. The medical teams wanted to save lives. The military needed to win the war. One British MO recalled casualties had to wait for the use of a trolley to transport them along the railway line. Artillery shells got first priority. Next came supplies for the military engineers, and then rations. Transporting the wounded to a CCS was the fourth priority.

Sometimes the system broke down under the weight of heavy casualties. Ypres, Belgium, was the site of several horrific battles. During one, the CCS filled quickly. Trains continued to dump loads of injured soldiers at the railhead and

Some hospital trains were managed by the Red Cross and used volunteer nurses.

surrounding fields. No one was available to meet or tend the wounded. It took four days to get all the wounded into tents and the dead to the cemetery. The CCS added a dressing station at the railhead to treat men as soon as they arrived. The British Royal Engineers, a corps that provided engineering and technical support, built new huts and installed electric lights. Space filled as soon as it was available.

NEVER ENOUGH TIME OR HELP

Treating patients was especially challenging because of the huge numbers and the severity of the wounds. Sometimes 100 or more patients arrived at the hospital at once. Dr. John Hayward, a British surgeon serving in France, described his overwhelming first experience, working 36 hours straight: "They come in such numbers that the tent is soon filled. Many are white and cold, and lie still and make no response, and those who do [say few words]. . . . I have had no instructions how to dispose of such numbers, or the method of procedure, but realize that they must be examined briefly and sorted, and sent to one or other of our hospital tents."[7]

At Souttar's Antwerp hospital, the most serious cases went straight into surgery or waited their turn in the great hall. Those who could walk went upstairs; those who could not stayed on the ground floor. "There was no use in putting up a notice 'House Full'; the men were wounded and they must be

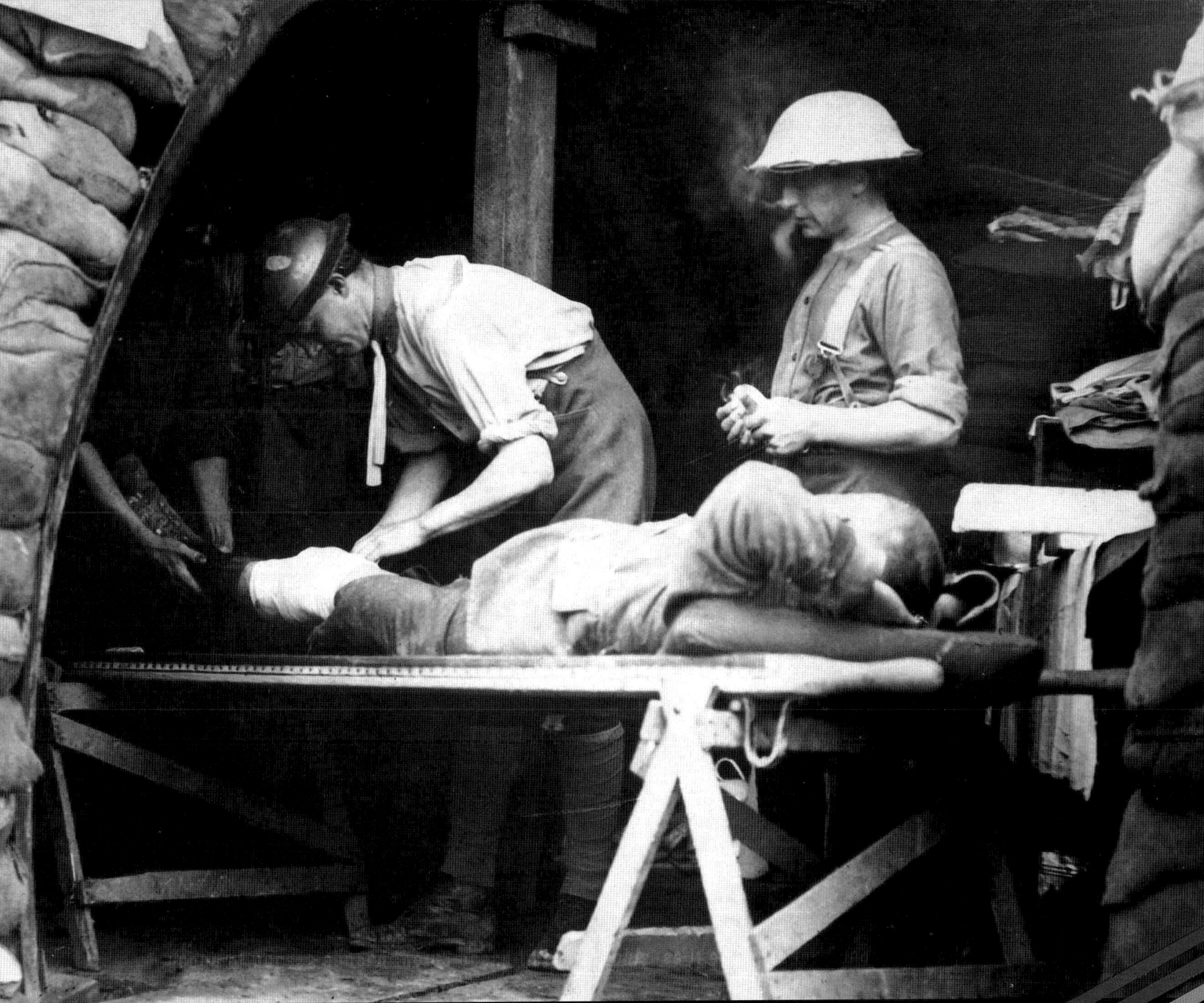

At a dressing station, the wounded were separated by triage into three categories.

attended to," Souttar wrote. "Sometimes we were hard put to it to find room for them all, but we always managed somehow, and we never refused admission to a single patient on the score of want of room."[8]

Even at the base hospitals, crowding was a problem. During the war, the military often enlisted local area hospitals or infirmaries for soldier care. Other schools and institutions volunteered their rooms and spaces. New hospitals were built as well, sometimes by the military and sometimes by volunteers. Elsie Maud Inglis, a British doctor, established two hospitals in France staffed by women.

In the United Kingdom, base hospitals had a capacity of 40,000 beds at the end of 1914. By the end of the war, they had expanded to hold 365,000 beds. The Berlin, Germany, area had 140 military hospitals by 1917. It could hold 20 times more patients than in the years before the war.[9]

VOLUNTEERS

In every country involved in the war, large numbers of doctors and nurses volunteered to serve. Often they supported the war effort and wanted to use their skills to work toward victory. Medical personnel also volunteered from countries that were not part of the war. Yet there were never enough doctors and nurses. On average, 15,000 to 20,000 people were wounded every day between all the areas of battle. On some days of heavy fighting, up to 100,000 people might be wounded.[10] Most medical personnel were not trained specifically for

ELSIE INGLIS

1864–1917

Elsie Maud Inglis spent the first 14 years of her life in India until her father retired and the family moved to Scotland. Inglis studied medicine at the Edinburgh School of Medicine for Women. She became a doctor, teacher, and founder of a maternity hospital staffed by women. She also helped establish the Scottish Women's Suffrage Federation, which fought for women's right to vote.

The outbreak of World War I turned Inglis's attention to helping the troops, and she suggested creating women's medical units. The British government was not interested, but France approved the idea. By December 1914, Inglis had a 200-bed hospital in place. She established another hospital in 1917 and also arranged for women's units to travel to battlefronts throughout Europe. Inglis served in Serbia, where she was captured and remained a prisoner of war for several months. After her release, she formed a new unit and headed it in Russia. She became ill and returned to England, where she died in 1917. She was buried with full military honors and was later honored by both the United Kingdom and Serbia.

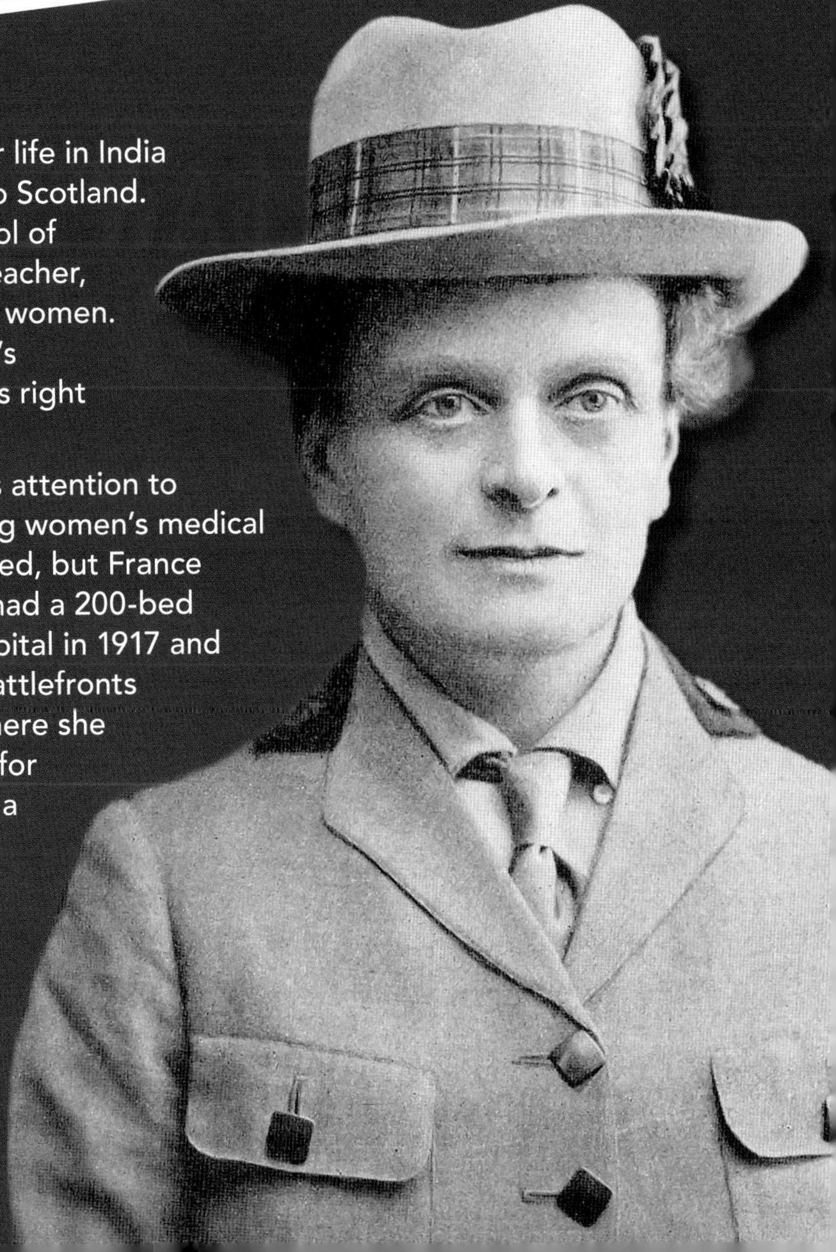

battlefield medicine. Despite poor equipment and insufficient time for proper training, they had to learn on the job.

Doctors and nurses were needed at home as well. At the start of the war, 300,000 men joined the British army in only two weeks.[11] All of those new recruits had to be examined and approved for fighting. That meant keeping doctors in the United Kingdom rather than moving them to the front. There were never enough doctors, nurses, or equipment.

In the United Kingdom, the War Office first decided to recruit young doctors who were not yet in practice. This allowed experienced doctors to stay at home to treat civilians. As the war continued, and some doctors died in the conflict, the War Office had to keep raising the age of doctors they recruited.

By 1916, the British could not find enough volunteers to fight and introduced a draft. However, doctors were exempt from the draft to avoid putting too much of a strain on health care at home. In France and Germany, medical personnel were subjected to the draft. This initially provided better medical care to those forces. The United States declared war on Germany on April 6, 1917. With the United States officially entered in the war, the US military sent doctors and nurses to help the British forces. Even before the United States officially entered the war, US doctors and nurses volunteered through the Red Cross.

As the war continued, more medical personnel were recruited, but many were not well qualified. Yet they had to deal with unfamiliar illnesses and injuries, sometimes complicated by extreme cold or heat. Throughout the war, medical personnel struggled to meet the demands placed on them by the battles. They could not always succeed. Still, as medical help moved closer to the front line, more soldiers survived wounds that would have previously been fatal.

CARING FOR ANIMALS

Many animals served during the war. Horses worked as cavalry mounts. Horses and mules hauled ambulances and supplies over difficult terrain. Dogs sniffed out wounded soldiers in the muddy trenches and battlefields. Veterinarians were needed to care for these animals. They detected and treated diseases, performed surgeries, and watched over the animals' recoveries. Mobile veterinary units evacuated wounded or sick animals to veterinary hospitals. In France, a typical veterinary hospital could house 2,000 patients. In the course of the war, 2.5 million animals were hospitalized in France. Two million of those were able to return for duty. In Egypt, some British hospitals specialized in camels.[12]

WORK OF THE RED CROSS

The International Committee of the Red Cross was founded in Switzerland in 1863. Its goal was, and is, to protect and help victims of war and other violence. Clara Barton, a US teacher and nurse, founded the American National Red Cross (ANRC) in 1881. In the next decade, the organization introduced programs in first aid, water safety, and public health nursing. When World War I broke out, the ANRC was a small organization. Still, within weeks it sent a ship with 117 surgeons and nurses to Europe to provide medical relief to casualties on both sides of the war. When the United States declared war against Germany in 1917, ANRC membership quickly grew. By the end of the war, the ANRC had more than 20 million adult and 11 million junior members.[13]

During World War I, more than 18,000 Red Cross nurses served with the US Army and Navy Nurse Corps. This included nurses who worked at US military camps, factories, and shipyards associated with the war effort. Many Red Cross nurses also served overseas, at base hospitals, aboard ships, or in the field. They served with both the US and British forces. The ANRC established 54 hospitals overseas, mainly in France, and another four in the United States. The Red Cross also helped civilians during the influenza pandemic.

Some Red Cross nurses stayed in Europe for several years after the war ended. They cared for injured soldiers or worked with civilians. The Red Cross ran schools and children's clinics, helping orphans, refugees, and others. Four hundred ANRC workers, including 296 nurses, lost their lives as a result of wartime activities.

Posters, such as this one that appeared in New York, urged women to join the Red Cross.

During World War I, splints such as the leg splint, *center*, helped save lives.

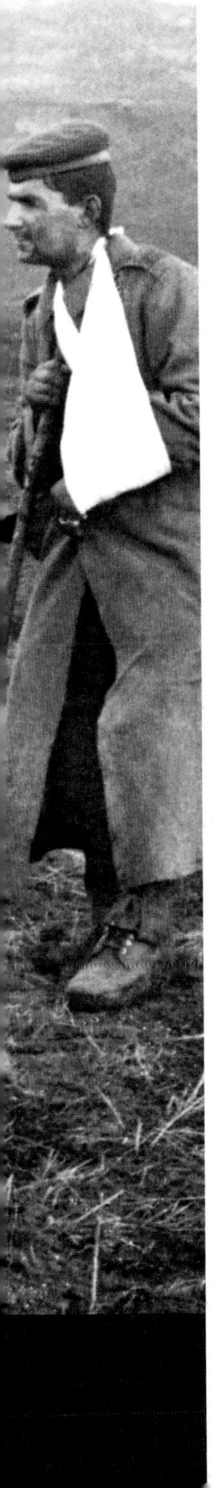

CHAPTER 3

ADVANCES IN SURGERY

Medical personnel on the front lines developed new techniques to save soldiers' lives. New equipment and practices were adapted more quickly and used more widely than during times of peace. During World War I, several medical advances became more common, including the use of blood transfusions and X rays in the field. Advances in anesthesia and the equipment to administer it also progressed greatly during and after the war.

Some improvements seem simple in retrospect. At the start of the war, 80 percent of patients with a broken femur died from the massive loss of blood. By 1916, 80 percent survived, thanks in part to a new type of splint that secured the broken leg.[1] The Thomas splint was invented in the late 1800s by Welsh surgeon Hugh Owen

Thomas. His surgeon nephew, Robert Jones, encouraged its use during World War I.

The splint kept patients alive long enough for surgery, but surgeons still faced challenging wounds. Bullets and shrapnel did not leave a clean break; rather, several inches of bone might be missing. Doctors began using steel plates to replace the missing portion of bone, attaching the plate to the remaining bone with steel screws. Despite worries that plates and screws would come loose or introduce infection, the system worked remarkably well.

BLOOD TRANSFUSIONS

Soldiers often suffered heavy blood loss from multiple injuries. Before they received help, they often spent hours wet, cold, and hungry, with their wounds becoming more painful. These factors made shock a common problem. Blood transfusions could save a patient in shock. Dr. Hayward marveled at the benefits: "The effect of transfusion was in some cases miraculous. I have seen men already like corpses, blanched and collapsed, pulseless and with just perceptible breathing, within two hours of transfusion sitting up in bed smoking, and exchanging jokes before they went to the operating table."[2]

The first blood transfusions happened in the 1600s. The British army was using blood transfusions at the start of World War I. However, only fresh blood could be used, by transferring the blood immediately from the donor to the patient. When the wounded started pouring in to hospitals, a large number of donors was needed to provide enough blood. Captain Oswald Robertson, a US Army doctor, established the first blood bank on the western front in 1917. He used sodium citrate, a kind of salt, to keep the blood from coagulating, or clotting. Blood could be kept chilled on ice for up to 28 days and transported where needed. Because it was often stored in glass bottles, it was not uncommon for them to break during transportation. Treating shock with blood transfusions continues today. Even sodium citrate is still used as an anticoagulant during blood donations.

BETTER BLOOD

The first blood transfusions happened in the 1600s, but it was not until 1907 that doctors started to understand blood types. Matching blood types makes transfusions more successful. However, during World War I, doctors often did not have the equipment needed to test blood types, or the time to do the testing. After the war, options for recruiting blood donors, and for testing and storing blood, improved. By World War II (1939–1945), blood transfusion was a standard practice.

SEEING INSIDE THE BODY

Once a patient's risk of shock was past, the surgeon could remove any bullets or shrapnel lodged in the soldier's body. X rays could show where these were. Without an X ray, some pieces could be missed until the site developed pain and infection, requiring additional surgeries. Although X rays had been used since 1896, they had been largely limited to a hospital setting. Famous physicist and chemist Marie Curie changed that. She convinced the French government to let her set up military radiology centers. She persuaded rich acquaintances to donate money and cars. Then she had automobile body shops turn the cars into vans that could haul the equipment. Manufacturers donated X ray machines. Curie had the first radiology van ready to go by October 1914. She eventually outfitted 20 vans, which soldiers nicknamed *petites Curies*, or "little Curies."

Curie had studied X rays but had not worked with medical X-ray machines. She learned how to use the equipment and drive a car, and she also studied anatomy and auto mechanics. Her 17-year-old daughter, Irène, and a military doctor accompanied her. They headed to the battlefront in the autumn of 1914 to provide X-ray services to the French army. A year later, Irène began installing machines on her own. Marie Curie also trained other women to work as radiological assistants. Approximately 150 women learned X-ray technology at her Radium Institute in Paris, France.

MARIE CURIE

Marie Curie was born Maria Sklodowska in Warsaw, Poland, in 1867. Although she was a top student, she could not attend the University of Warsaw, which only admitted men. She worked as a tutor and governess while studying in her spare time and took classes through a secret informal university. She finally moved to Paris to study and earned master's degrees in physics and math. She married French physicist Pierre Curie, and they had two daughters. Pierre eventually joined Marie in her work on radioactivity. Marie became the first woman to win a Nobel Prize when she won the award in physics in 1903. She won a second Nobel Prize in chemistry in 1911, making her the only woman to win the award in two fields.

Marie Curie drives one of her X-ray units in 1914.

After the war, Curie offered radiology classes to US soldiers who were waiting for passage home.

MANAGING PAIN

From the patient's perspective, one of the most important parts of medical care is managing pain. Doctors provided morphine to treat pain and had anesthesia for use during surgery. Chloroform was commonly used at the beginning of the war. Getting the correct dosage was tricky. Too much could be fatal, but not enough meant the patient could wake up. In that dreamlike state, patients relived the battle, thrashing and screaming. Few doctors specialized in anesthetics before the war. Instead, surgeons worked in teams and traded off between operating and providing the anesthetic.

The demands of wartime encouraged some people to specialize in anesthesia. These anesthetists also helped develop treatments for shock. Geoffrey Marshall, a British doctor, studied the effects of different anesthetic agents while working at a CCS. The type and amount of anesthesia given affected the level of shock a patient suffered. Chloroform was thought to contribute more to shock, so ether and nitrous oxide, sometimes combined with oxygen, became more popular.

Nitrous oxide–oxygen anesthesia was expensive and difficult to administer. However, it took action quickly and recovery was faster and easier.

MORPHINE

The drug opium comes from the unripe seeds of a flowering poppy. It has been used for thousands of years to control pain. In the 1700s and 1800s, opium was used for pain relief and as a recreational drug. Morphine, a component extracted from opium, worked even better for pain relief. In 1853, the introduction of the hypodermic needle, which injects substances under the skin, allowed the injection of the drug directly into the bloodstream. Although accidental deaths sometimes occurred when too much was administered, morphine and elixir of opium were used as painkillers during World War I. Morphine is still used today for intense pain, but opium and morphine are both highly addictive.

Unfortunately, supply did not keep up with demand. Eventually the American National Red Cross (ANRC) raised funds to build a nitrous oxide plant in France. It could produce 125,000 gallons (473,000 L) of the gas in eight hours. New methods of administering anesthesia were also developed, including the use of machines and tubes inserted in the windpipe.

Local anesthetic and spinal injections were also given for injuries in certain body parts. Souttar described the benefits of spinal anesthesia: "With the injection of a minute quantity of fluid into the spine all sensation disappears up to the level of the arms, and, provided [the wounded] cannot see what is going on, any operation below that level can be carried out without the patient knowing anything about it at all. It is rather uncanny at first to see a patient lying smoking a cigarette and reading the paper whilst on the other side of a screen a big operation is in progress."[3]

Many advances in medicine were made during the war. However, they were not always widely applied. Equipment was often in short supply, and doctors and nurses barely had time to care for patients, let alone learn new techniques. Still, some of the advances that became more widespread helped save lives, during and after the war.

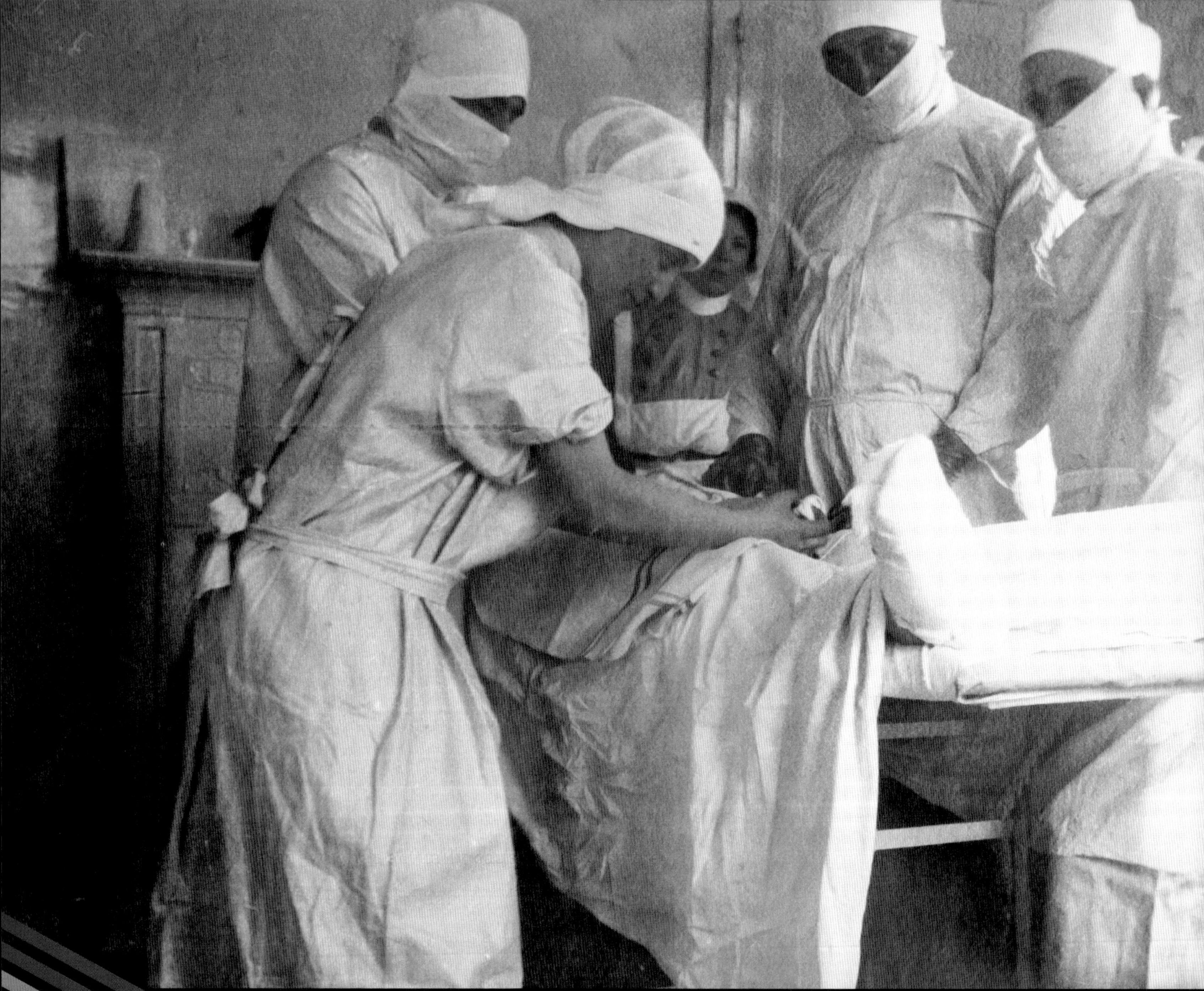

A French medical team prepares to amputate a soldier's foot before infection overtakes the soldier's body.

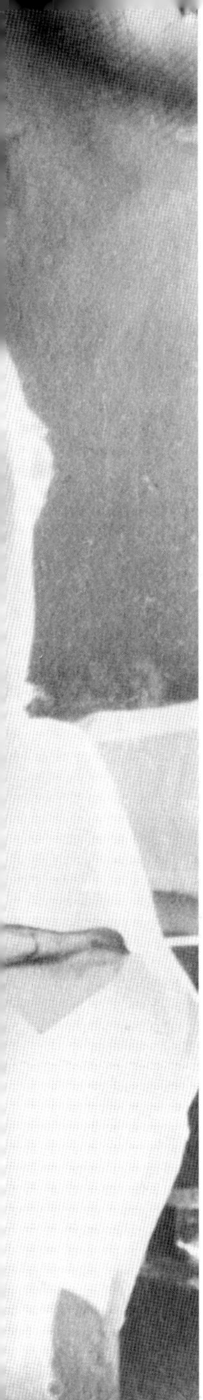

CHAPTER 4

WARDING OFF INFECTION

Splinting broken bones and stopping blood loss were merely the beginning of treatment for battlefield wounds. In Europe, soldiers were often fighting on farm fields fertilized by manure. Wounds easily became infected, causing gangrene, the death of soft tissue due to a bacterial infection or lack of blood flow. Surgeon Sir Anthony Bowlby noted, "It is practically true that every gunshot wound of this war in France and Belgium is more or less infected at the moment of its infliction."[1] And because reaching treatment could take hours or even days, infections could set in well before treatment. In the early war years, many limbs were amputated to remove infected tissue before it could take over the rest of the body. Even this had a poor success rate. Approximately 38 percent of gangrene victims died within two days of reaching the CCS.[2]

Before the war, most wounds received a simple treatment. Any obvious foreign bodies were removed and the site was flushed with a cleanser. The wound was left open to drain or was packed with gauze. Several doctors experimented with different methods in the first months of the war. They discovered better results with debridement. With the method of debridement, all damaged tissue around the wound is cut away, leaving a clean edge. Then the wound is sealed. This helps reduce infections.

Cleaning wounds and keeping them clean was imperative. In 1916, Alexis Carrel, a French surgeon, and Henry Drysdale Dakin, an English chemist, developed the Carrel–Dakin fluid. This antiseptic solution was used to flush a wound, where it helped separate dead and living tissue. At first, the solution had to be mixed onsite with exactly the right amount of each ingredient. Otherwise it would either be too irritating or would fail

KILLING INFECTIONS

Antibiotics are powerful drugs that can cure patients with deadly infections. Penicillin, the first antibiotic, was discovered in 1928. It was not widely used until the 1940s, but it was an important medicine in World War II. In World War I, with no antibiotics, 18 percent of patients with bacterial pneumonia died. In World War II, that number fell to less than 1 percent, thanks to penicillin.[3] Another important class of drugs, sulfa drugs, gained use at approximately the same time as penicillin. Penicillin and sulfa drugs are still used, along with newer antibiotics. Doctors in World War I had to do without these powerful medicines.

to sterilize the wound. Then Johnson & Johnson, a US company, began mass producing the solution and the equipment needed to administer it. This helped reduce mistakes. Edinburgh University Solution of Lime (EUSOL) was a British version of the antiseptic. Several other solutions were also used to disinfect wounds. Then gauze soaked in the solution was wrapped around the wound.

These solutions not only saved lives but also allowed more injured soldiers to keep their limbs. Advances in wound treatment during World War I led to a better understanding of infections. This encouraged more hygienic practices and better future treatments.

Whereas doctors were generally responsible for immediate wound care, nurses had to change the dressings and keep wounds clean as they healed. This was not easy under the conditions of the battlefield. Ideally, equipment and dressings were sterilized in boiling water before use. In reality, it was sometimes impossible to boil water, or even to get enough water. Then unsterilized dressings had to be used, hopefully with some kind of disinfectant.

NURSES AT WORK

Although military nurses had originally been male, that changed around the beginning of the 1900s. For example, in the United States, the Army Nurse Corps was formed in 1901, and then only women could serve as military nurses. Men could work as orderlies, doing many of the same duties but for less pay. In many

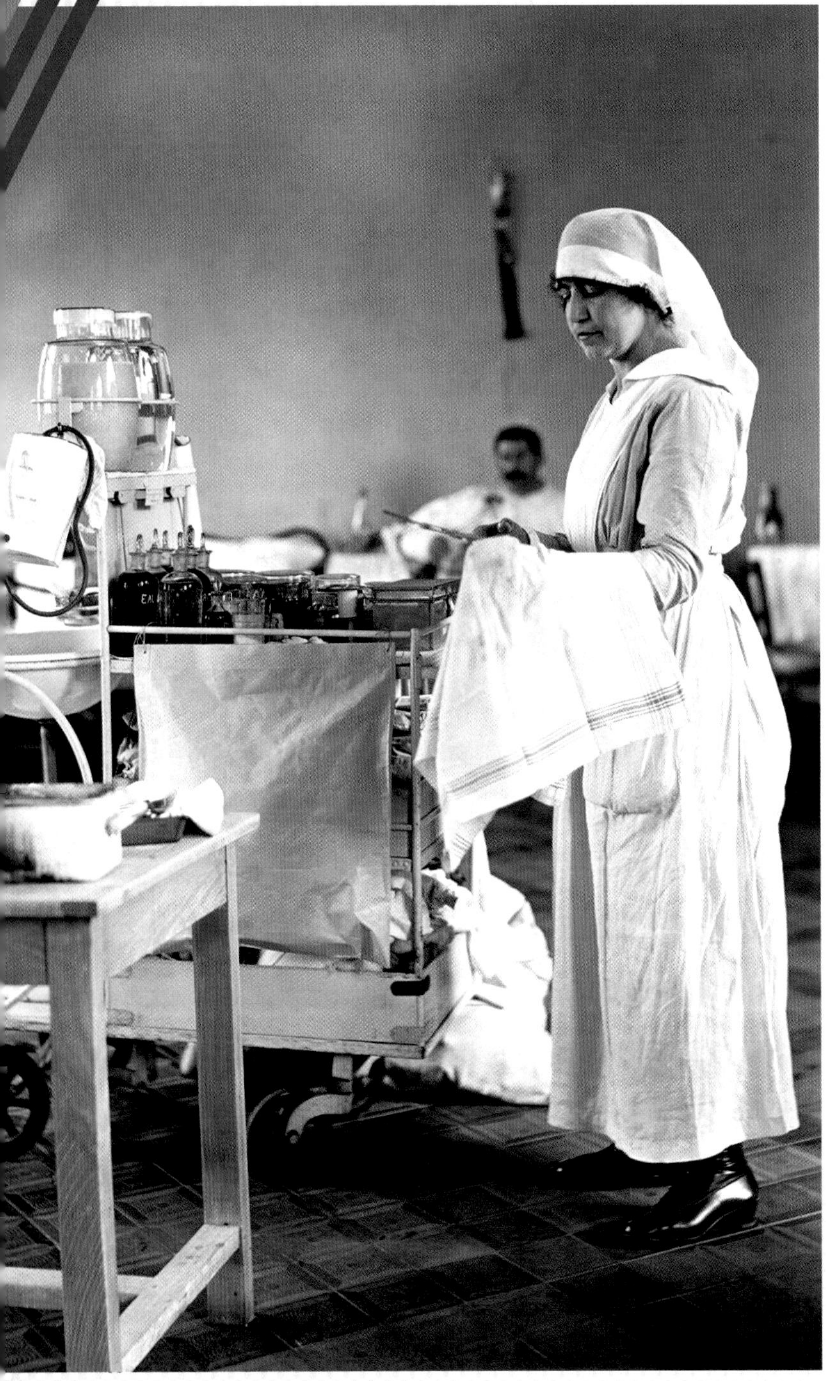

countries, men who were unable to fight might work as orderlies, but healthy men were usually sent into battle. Many people thought war was no place for women, even nurses. Before World War I, nurses were typically kept away from the battlefield, working at hospitals safely away from the fighting. Women did not fight in World War I, but they did serve as nurses and ambulance drivers. In some cases, they worked at the front lines.

Nurses proved themselves capable of handling the horrors of war and working in all conditions. Some even sought out the toughest positions. Nurse Winifred Kenyon wanted to be as close to the war as possible. She was stationed at a CCS in the French countryside, a vast tent city. The wind blew constantly and sometimes

A US nurse sterilizes equipment.

ripped down rows of tents. During winter, nurses slept in their uniforms and woke to frozen food and supplies. In spring, rain turned paths into swamps. The nurses checked charts, changed dressings, administered medicine, washed laundry, and comforted those who had lost limbs. And when a patient died, nurses often wrote to the soldier's family, sharing last words and messages and letting the family know the location of the grave.

HONORED NURSE

Lenah Sutcliffe Higbee joined the US Navy Nurse Corps when it was first established in 1908. She was soon appointed chief nurse and later superintendent of the Nurse Corps. She helped pioneer a new nurse training program to meet the demand for more qualified nurses. Higbee was the first living woman to be awarded the Navy Cross, which she received for her work during World War I. She was also the first woman to have a naval ship named after her.

In several wards, the nurses worked without doctors. Because of the shortage of surgeons, nurses sometimes had to do work beyond their normal training. They administered anesthesia and closed off amputated limbs. They determined which patients had no chance of survival and which should receive help next.

RISKING AND GIVING THEIR LIVES

US military nurses served during the war even before the United States sent fighting troops. US Army nurses helped the British establish six base hospitals. After the United States officially joined the war, US Army nurses served in many

countries throughout Europe and in Puerto Rico, Hawaii, and the Philippines. More than 10,000 served, and 200 died in service. Approximately 1,700 US Navy nurses served, and 36 died during the war.[4] Most of the nurses who died were the victims of influenza, which they contracted from patients during an epidemic toward the end of the war.

Nurses treated all kinds of injuries, both physical and emotional. Often they faced harsh weather and water shortages. Julia Stimson, chief nurse of the Army Nurse Corps, described the difficulties at Rouen, France: "Our people at home would marvel to see what fine work can be done when all the water used has to be heated on top of a small oil stove and all the instruments boiled the same way."[5]

Nurses often penned letters home for injured or dying soldiers.

Nurses worked in many challenging conditions, including onboard hospital ships. Medical personnel on hospital ships faced dangers from enemy ships, submarines, and mines. German submarines and mines sank at least 15 British hospital ships. When Australian forces landed at Gallipoli in Turkey, hospital ships were in the midst of the action. Nurse Alice Kitchen wrote about being caught in the crossfire: "The shells fired in return whistled and shrieked as they passed over or beside us & made huge splashes as they fell, often near the destroyers. Our anchor always gets hauled up & we get a wriggle on, on these occasions." Nurse Hilda Samsing described how "stray bullets pattered on board like raindrops after a shower."[6]

NURSERY MAIDS

Many soldiers serving overseas married local women. Australian soldiers alone brought 11,000 family members home. Nurses serving on these transport ships had to add maternity and infant care to their roles. Whereas some enjoyed the work, others complained. Nurse Jessie Tomlins wrote about traveling with 790 wives and children on a transport ship. "We have to act as nurserymaids on those family Boats, mind the babies while the mothers dine etc—that's hardly the job we came for."[7]

SERVING ON A HOSPITAL SHIP

Doctors and nurses working on hospital ships faced additional difficulties. Equipment had to be tied down or it would scatter with the rolling of the ship. Ella Tucker, an Australian nurse, wrote that on rough days, she had to "pack all our mixtures & surgical things in the cupboards round with sheets, & tie the dressing tables with bandages to the various supports in the ward."[8] Coal embers and dust blew in from the ship's funnels, and surgical tools might have to be sterilized over small lamp flames. On board ships, water was in short supply, even for drinking, let alone washing wounds.

When the hospital constantly moved, even simple procedures took more time and effort. May Tiltonde, an Australian nurse, noted, "There were days we could not measure medicines or fill hot water bags unless we had the help of the boys to steady us."[9]

They also suffered from the climate, especially in the hot tropics. During evacuation drills, doctors and nurses moved bedridden patients to the lifeboats. The nurses removed any wooden leg splints. Otherwise, if the patients wound up in the sea, the splints might float and turn the patients head down in the water.

A group of nurses aboard the US ocean liner *St. Louis* as it embarks for Europe in 1915

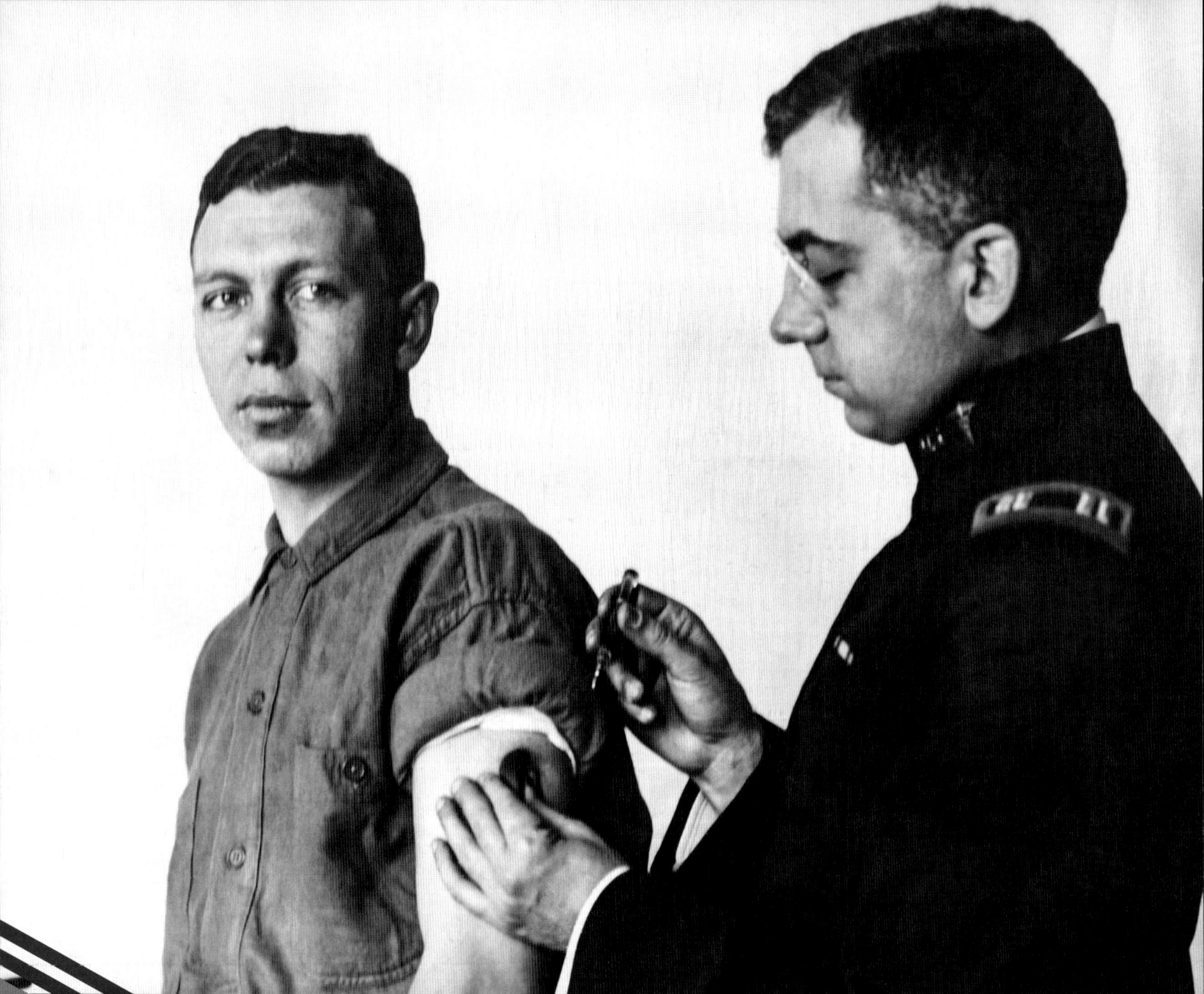

As disease spread quickly in trenches, many recruits and soldiers received vaccinations.

CHAPTER 5

THE WAR AGAINST DISEASE

One of the biggest wartime killers is typically not the enemy. Instead, it is contagious diseases. Although battlefield wounds are frightening and dangerous, even uninjured men can contract deadly diseases. In fact, before World War I, more soldiers died from disease than from wounds received during fighting.

By World War I, military doctors had learned about the importance of good hygiene. After the Spanish-American War (1898), the US Army Medical Department did intensive research on field sanitation, water purification, garbage disposal, and insect and parasite control. Carl R. Darnall, who had served the US Army as an assistant surgeon, discovered liquid chlorine could purify

CARL R. DARNALL

1867–1941

Carl R. Darnall of Texas joined the US Army as an assistant surgeon in 1896. He served in Cuba during the Spanish-American War. He then worked on a hospital ship and ran a military hospital in the Philippines. After serving during the Boxer Rebellion of 1900 in China, Darnall became a professor at the Army Medical School in Washington. There he discovered liquid chlorine could purify water. He developed a water filter, which was then used by the army. His discovery was later applied to city water supplies and is now used all around the world.

During World War I, Darnall, who was then a lieutenant colonel, directed the Finance and Supply Division of the Surgeon General's office. He was awarded the Distinguished Service Medal for his work in ensuring medical supplies were available for the troops. In the course of his career, he wrote many papers, contributing to surgery and chemistry.

water, and he developed a water filter. Military doctors had in fact contributed many advances to medicine. The British army used an early version of a typhoid vaccine during the Second Boer War in Africa (1899–1902). Major Frederick F. Russell of the US Army Medical School developed a typhoid vaccine based on the one used by the British army.

US military doctors also studied other tropical diseases during and after the Spanish-American War. US Army research into yellow fever in 1900 proved mosquitoes spread the disease. This led to mosquito control programs to prevent the disease in tropical outposts.

By 1914, experts understood diseases could be caused by viruses, bacteria, and other microorganisms. Infectious diseases could then be spread by contact with someone who had the disease. However, many older doctors had studied medicine before these theories were accepted. Some did not believe microbes caused disease. Still, a general understanding of the causes of disease helped save lives.

VACCINATIONS

Personal cleanliness and sanitary surroundings are important to preventing the spread of disease. Unfortunately, this is difficult to achieve during a war. Vaccination was a simpler answer for some diseases, helping prevent people who had been vaccinated from getting the disease in the first place.

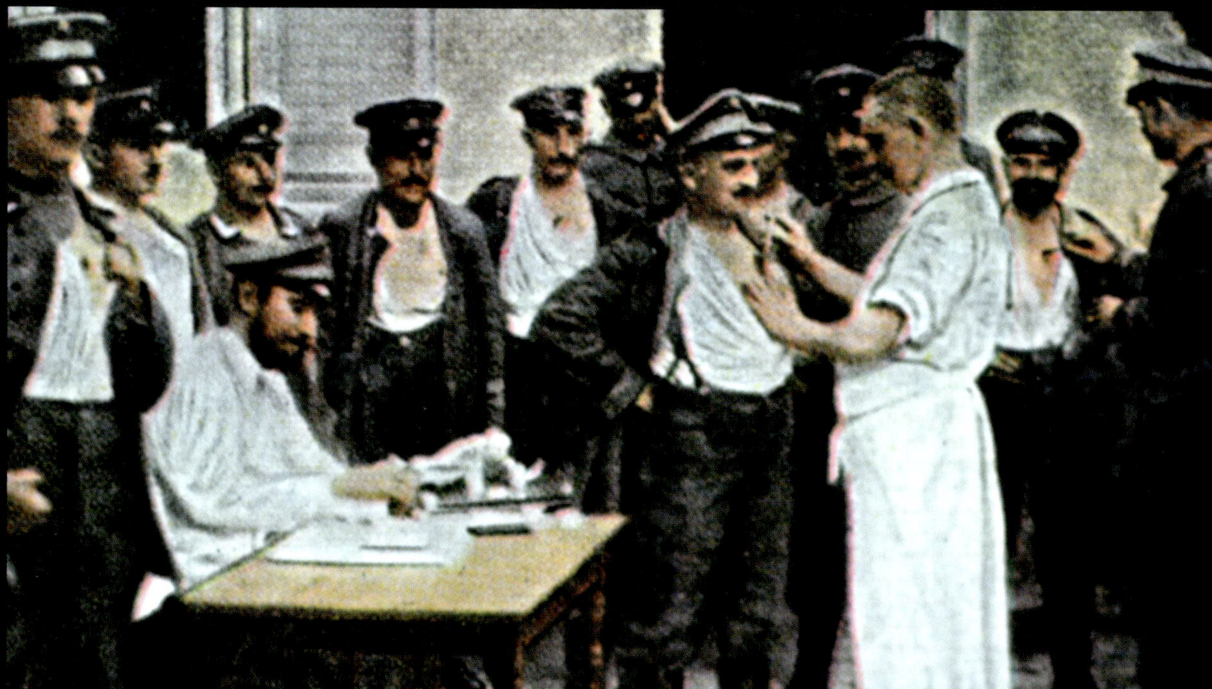

German soldiers receive vaccinations.

Vaccination practices varied from country to country. In Germany, soldiers could be required to get vaccinations. In the United Kingdom, any vaccination was voluntary. This was in part because in Germany young men were required to sign up for military service, whereas the United Kingdom did not institute a draft until 1916. British volunteers were given more choices than German draftees were. British war propaganda even claimed Germany's forced vaccination policy proved how authoritarian the country was. Yet in reality, most

British soldiers were vaccinated, if only because of the encouragement to do so. Those who refused vaccination had a much higher rate of illness. All US troops were vaccinated against some diseases.

Vaccines existed against typhoid, tetanus, cholera, plague, rabies, and anthrax, although not all were widely used. For many other diseases, vaccines did not exist. A measles vaccine would not be developed for several decades. Measles, a serious and potentially deadly disease when it struck adults, could spread quickly in the close quarters soldiers shared. Nurses attempted to stop the spread by isolating patients and those who came in contact with them.

Different countries and climates provided different disease challenges. British, French, and German armies fighting in Macedonia suffered greatly from malaria, which can cause headaches, fever, and vomiting, and can even be deadly. There is still no vaccine for malaria on the market. Eighty percent of French troops posted to Macedonia came down with the disease.[1] Armies fighting around the Mediterranean also suffered from malaria.

A typhus epidemic hit Serbia early in the war in November 1914. No vaccine was available against typhus, which caused delirium, rashes, sores, and potentially death. The country had fewer than 400 doctors, 126 of whom died from the disease. Serbia had few hospitals, few nurses, and few medicines. Seventy thousand Serbian troops died from typhus fever, along with 120,000

Serbian civilians and 30,000 Austrian prisoners of war.[2] Fear of the disease was the only thing that prevented Austria from taking over the helpless country.

HUNGRY AND CROWDED

As the war raged on, conditions became even worse. Initially, only healthy young men were sent into battle. As more and more soldiers were needed, standards dropped. Soldiers who previously would have been considered mentally or physically unfit to serve joined the ranks. One wartime cartoon showed a doctor approving a skeleton fit for service. More doctors and nurses were also needed, and the newer ones were sometimes not well qualified.

Hunger and poor nutrition can contribute to illness, and keeping an army fed is difficult. The amount and quality of food decreased as the war continued. Soldiers on the western front ate mainly canned corned beef, bread (which was often stale), and biscuits. As even those products came in short supply, the soldiers received mainly vegetable soup, perhaps with small chunks of horsemeat. Bread might be made with ground turnips, and kitchen staff scavenged for local edible weeds.

In September 1915, an Australian soldier stationed at Gallipoli described the daily menu in a letter home to his parents. Breakfast was a six-inch (15 cm) piece of bacon, hard biscuits, and tea. Sometimes they also got a loaf of bread.

At midday, they had nothing but sweetened tea. The final meal was canned beef stew.

Crowding was also a problem. US Surgeon General William C. Gorgas stated, "We know perfectly well that we can control pneumonia absolutely if we could avoid crowding the men, but it is not practicable in military life to avoid this crowding."[3]

Illness often struck even before soldiers reached the battlefield. Transport ships brought soldiers from distant countries such as Australia and Canada to the war zone. Epidemics of measles and mumps were common during these voyages. Flu and pneumonia could also spread quickly.

Food rarely reached the trenches hot.

BY THE NUMBERS

The number of people killed during World War I is not certain, but estimates have been made:

- 6 million civilians
- 10 million military personnel (4 million Central powers and 6 million Allied forces)
- 60 percent to 70 percent of the military deaths were from combat (30 percent to 40 percent from disease).
- Between the Allies and Central powers, approximately 65 million troops served in the war. More than one-half of them, more than 37 million, were killed, wounded, or missing by the end.[5]

Medical personnel, especially nurses, were exposed to every illness as they treated patients. Many grew sick, yet they had to continue caring for their patients. Helen Bulovsky, a US nurse, wrote in a letter to her parents, "I am in bed with everything imaginable on, even a muffler around my neck. I have had another attack of quincy [a throat infection]. . . . The first 3 days my throat was swollen. I remained on duty. Outside my throat felt fine and the boys need every little bit of our attention available. By night I couldn't talk so I had to go to bed."[4]

Some diseases require closer contact to spread. Soldiers were typically far from home, lonely, and sometimes bored. Meanwhile, many local women lost the support of husbands and other family members. Prostitution became one of the few ways local women could support themselves. In these conditions, venereal diseases (VDs)—known now as sexually transmitted diseases (STDs)—such as syphilis and gonorrhea spread quickly. Approximately 5 percent of British soldiers became infected with VDs. These illnesses were seldom fatal but required up to a month of treatment. At one point, an estimated 11,000 British soldiers were hospitalized with VDs, taking men away from the fighting.[6]

A DEADLY FLU

Illness was always a problem during the war, but in 1918, Spanish Flu became a disaster. It started like an ordinary cold, but it developed quickly, sometimes killing people within a few hours. It affected civilians and soldiers alike, but it spread especially quickly in close quarters, such as the trenches. There was no vaccine and no antibiotics to treat influenza.

It is believed the disease arose in China and spread to the United States. The flu broke out in 14 large US training camps in the spring of 1918, but the disease did not yet seem particularly deadly. The flu struck hard as the American Expeditionary Forces were preparing for their first big offensive against the Germans. Approximately one-quarter of the army, more than 1 million men, came down with the flu. Almost 30,000 died even before reaching France.[7] And US troops brought the flu to Europe.

Troops on both sides of the conflict were affected in Europe. For a few months, deaths from disease outnumbered deaths from combat. Because the United States joined the war late, as the influenza epidemic began, more US troops died overall from disease than in combat.

Soldiers gargle salt water, which was believed to prevent influenza.

Infectious diseases spread easily, especially among wounded or sick patients who had poor immunity, or protection against disease. Doctors could do little for flu or pneumonia except keep patients comfortable. They also tracked the disease, ran tests, and wrote detailed reports. These studies later helped researchers understand the spread of disease.

The end of the war did not see the end of disease. Wartime conditions encouraged the spread of disease in civilian populations. British troops with malaria went home to southern England, where it was not known at that time. Throughout Europe, people were starving and often did not have access to clean water. Several diseases spread more widely than they had before the war. In Germany, 97,000 people died from tuberculosis in 1914. In 1918, 148,000 people died from the disease. Three million people, mainly in refugee camps, died of typhus.[8] Soldiers who went home carried the Spanish Flu to civilian populations around the world. In the months after the war, diseases still killed many soldiers and civilians.

SPANISH FLU

Spanish Flu got its name because Spain was one of the first countries to widely report the disease. The sickness was first reported on March 11, 1918, and had spread around the world by June. Although many illnesses are more severe among children and the elderly, Spanish Flu had a higher death rate among adults younger than age 50. Approximately one-half of the people in the world contracted the flu, and an estimated 40 million or more people died.[9] With so many doctors and nurses in the military, some civilian areas had no medical care. The flu rampaged until late spring of 1919. Occasional cases cropped up for several decades, but it became largely harmless.

Soldiers often killed vermin, such as rats, that frequented the trenches and carried diseases.

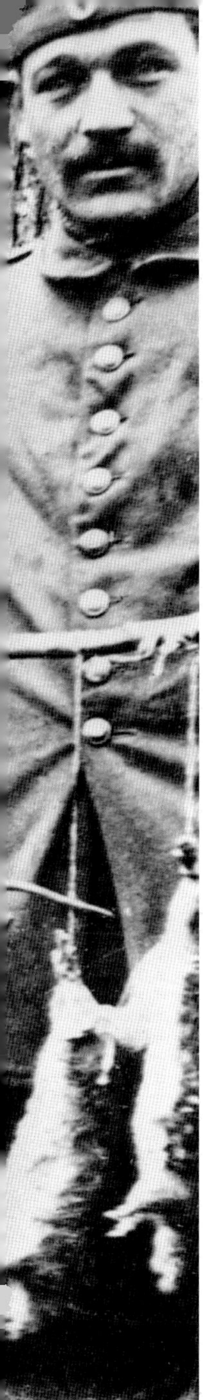

CHAPTER 6

TRENCH WARFARE

Although many diseases affected the general population, soldiers living in and fighting from the trenches suffered from diseases seldom seen elsewhere. Trenches often flooded, filling with mud, overflow from latrines, and rotting bodies. Vermin such as rats and lice were a constant torment. In these conditions, disease quickly spread, including unfamiliar diseases that came to be called trench fever, trench foot, and trench mouth.

Trench fever baffled doctors when they first saw it. Patients came in with headaches, dizziness, lower back and shin pain, and stiffness down the front of the thighs. The disease typically kept soldiers away from battle for three months. Although most soldiers did not mind the rest time, some soldiers had long-lasting effects from the disease after the war. More important at the time, the military lost fighters and filled valuable hospital beds. Among British, French, and Belgian soldiers, an estimated 500,000 came down with trench fever.[1]

Was this a new disease or an old one showing itself in a new way? At first people were not sure. Pathologists in mobile laboratories examined hundreds of cases. Finally, most experts agreed the disease was new. Soldiers already called the condition trench fever, so that became its official name.

Recognizing the disease was only the beginning. Symptoms lasted for a few days, went away, and came back. This trend was similar to malaria, which was known to be transmitted by mosquitoes. Doctors debated whether fleas, lice, or rodents, all of which were common in the trenches, could be the transmitters. Some doctors even thought climate or stress caused the sickness. By the end of 1916, lice had been identified as the disease carrier. Still no one knew what actually caused the disease. Finally, two years after the first case of the fever, a tiny bacteria found in lice feces was shown to be the problem.

Many treatments were tried with limited success. The best option was controlling the lice through cleanliness. However, soldiers in the trenches were

BLOCKING TRENCH FEVER

The United Kingdom was determined to not let trench fever affect the civilian population at home. Therefore, stations were set up in France to kill any lice soldiers might be carrying. Soldiers could not return home until their clothing had been disinfected. This kept the disease from spreading to civilians in the United Kingdom. However, the disease has reemerged in recent decades.

German soldiers remove lice from their uniforms.

lucky to get a bath every two weeks. Their uniforms also had to be sterilized because the lice hid in the seams. Early steam sterilizers, large machines drawn by horses, could not handle the demand. Late in the war, a hot air system worked better. One successful option was developed separately by the British and the French. A chemical paste rubbed into uniform seams killed lice in a few hours.

TRENCH FOOT

Another disease of the trenches, trench foot, came from the cold, wet conditions. Soldiers sometimes had to stand in cold water or mud for days at a time. This

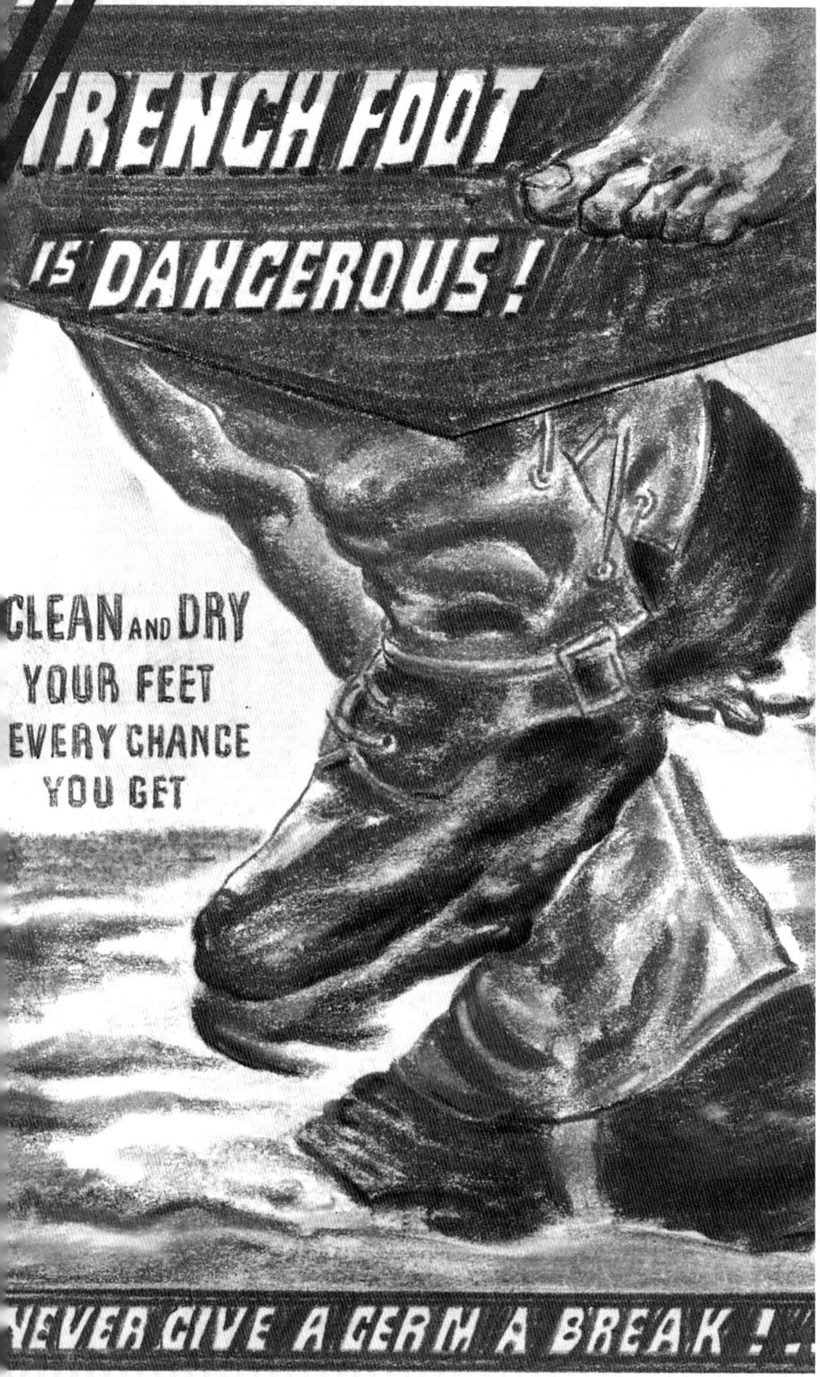

could reduce blood circulation to the feet. Swelling, numbness, and pain resulted. Infections often then set in. Poor diet and exhaustion contributed to the disease. Even mild cases of trench foot could take weeks or months of recovery. In more serious cases, toes or even the entire foot might develop gangrene, turning black and shriveling. In the worst cases, the feet had to be amputated. Trench foot also made patients susceptible to tetanus, a disease fatal within 48 hours.

The first cases of trench foot appeared in the winter of 1914. It was quickly recognized as a disease similar to frostbite and is now called nonfreezing cold injury. Treatment involved thoroughly cleaning the feet and keeping

Soldiers were urged to keep their feet as dry as possible.

them elevated. Doctors were warned not to amputate right away, as sometimes damaged feet recovered from gangrene.

Trench foot is best prevented by keeping the feet and socks clean and dry. However, that was often not possible in the trenches. Soldiers often did not have dry socks to change into, and boots were sometimes not removed for days or even weeks. Soldiers who could not properly air their feet were given foot powders or grease to reduce moisture.

Perhaps the most important measure was making the trenches more comfortable. Proper drainage kept trenches drier. When full drainage was impossible, wooden boards were laid down so troops could move without slogging through wet mud. Some lucky soldiers had charcoal braziers, metal pans for holding live coals, to help fight off the cold.

Rotating soldiers out of the trenches more often also helped. In the first winter of the war, troops often stayed in a trench for several weeks. As new reinforcements arrived, the time spent

UNPREPARED

At the start of the war, one of every three soldiers under British command in France was from India. Other colonial troops came from Africa and Southeast Asia. Many of these men had never experienced the extreme cold they found in Europe. Most did not have proper clothing or footwear for rain and snow, making them especially susceptible to frostbite and trench foot. A wounded Indian soldier wrote, "In this sinful country, it rains very much and also snows, and many men have been frost-bitten. . . . All the men will be finished here."[2] In addition, colonial troops had often not been exposed to European illnesses, making them more susceptible.

in the front trenches was reduced to 48 to 72 hours at a time, rotating between other stations.

MOUTH PROBLEMS

Trench mouth was a painful infection of the gums. The gums became infected when the normal bacteria balance was thrown off, often by poor nutrition, poor oral hygiene, smoking, or stress. The disease was known before World War I, but the rough conditions of the trenches made it especially common there. Many soldiers did not even try to keep up with oral hygiene. The disease was painful but not deadly. Today, the condition would be treated with antibiotics. During World War I, hydrogen peroxide was applied to the gums as a cleanser. This helped remove dead gum tissue.

LAND AND SEA

Battles at the western front were fought largely from the trenches. In other areas, the war was more mobile, but every army faced harsh conditions. For example, the Middle East offered extreme heat, water shortages, and rough terrain. Heatstroke was a common problem in the Middle East, where even temperatures in the shade could rise above 120 degrees Fahrenheit (49°C). Heatstroke also struck both patients and many members of the crew on one hospital ship voyage. Nurse Gladys Larkan described the challenge: "As fast as we could get the worst cases into ice packs & administer stimulants, other patients would collapse, their temperatures being anything up to 110°F [43°C] or as high as the thermometer would register."[3] In four days, 21 patients died from heatstroke.

During previous wars, few if any dentists had been available to soldiers. Any treatment was provided by general surgeons. A few months into World War I, 12 British dental surgeons were sent to CCSs. By May 1916, dentists traveled in ambulances fitted with mobile surgeries. They could then treat soldiers in the field so the men could return to fighting right away. By 1918, more than 800 dentists were serving in the British army. Each of the Allied armies in France had a mobile unit. These dentists extracted teeth, repaired damaged teeth, and dealt with injuries to the mouth area. The success of this system led to the United Kingdom's Army Dental Corps in 1921.

Stress, poor diet, and poor hygiene contribute to many diseases. The trenches thus became the ideal climate for illness to spread. Studying conditions such as trench fever helped doctors understand how such diseases spread and learn how to stop them. This led to more hygienic practices in base hospitals. The hygiene practices adopted in World War I to slow the spread of disease helped build the systems hospitals use today.

Chemical warfare in the form of phosgene gas caused suffocation, as shown in this photo staged by the US Army Engineer Corps to illustrate its effects.

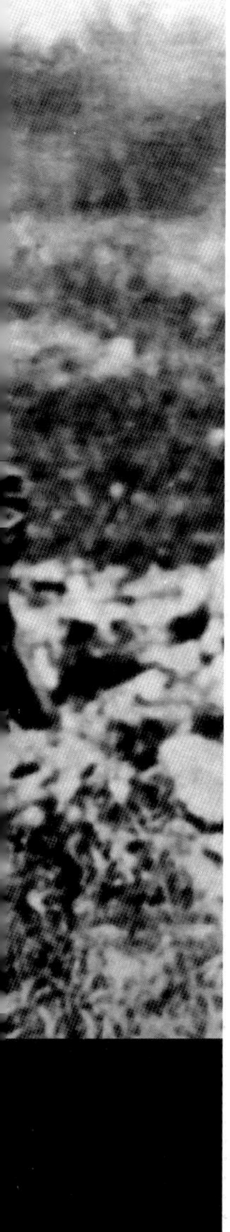

CHAPTER 7

THE CHEMISTS' WAR

Armies fighting in the trenches struggled to gain even a few hundred yards of ground. As the war dragged on, both sides looked for new weapons to make progress. The French used tear gas grenades starting in 1914. The British and Germans also began working on chemical weapons. These early weapons were designed to weaken rather than kill, and they were not very successful.

On April 22, 1915, approximately ten months into the war, the Germans introduced a new chemical weapon. A special German army unit set up more than 6,000 steel cylinders along their trenches at Ypres. They opened the valves to release chlorine gas, which quickly drifted downwind, across the French trenches. The Germans had expected the gas to drive soldiers out of their trenches, where the Germans could kill them with other weapons.

Instead, the poisonous gas quickly killed more than 1,000 French and Algerian soldiers and wounded another 4,000.[1]

Chlorine gas reacts with water in the body's airways. It forms an acid, causing swelling that can lead to suffocation. A British soldier described the fear and panic of the soldiers who survived long enough to flee: "Then there staggered into our midst French soldiers, blinded, coughing, chests heaving, faces an ugly purple color, lips speechless with agony, and behind them in the gas soaked trenches, we learned that they had left hundreds of dead and dying comrades."[2] Chemical weapons had been used successfully on the battlefield for the first time.

By mid-1915, armies on both sides were using chlorine gas. Within a year, they had added phosgene, another gas that targets the respiratory system, to make the mixture even more deadly. Chemical weapons did not actually have a high fatality rate, but they were a source of terror.

CHEMICAL WEAPON THREATS

International agreements in 1899 and 1907 forbade the wartime use of poison or poisonous weapons. These agreements were ignored by forces on both sides during World War I. After the war, international meetings tried to limit or abolish chemical weapons. In 1925, an international treaty called the Geneva Protocol outlawed the use of poisonous gases. However, many countries continued research on chemical weapons. During World War II, many countries, including the United States, used chemical weapons. Although they were used in combat less than in World War I, hundreds of thousands of civilians died from chemical weapons. Chemical weapons continue to be a threat today.

Poison gas was feared because it could be used on soldiers in the trenches even when no attack was happening, and because victims suffered days of agony before death. Because it was hard to control, civilians also suffered and died from it. If the wind changed, the gas could even blow back on the army that released it.

Although chemical gases did not kill large numbers, they did remove troops from the battlefield. The recovery period was long, approximately 45 days for phosgene gas and 60 days for chlorine.

GAS FATALITIES

By some estimates, approximately 90,000 soldiers were killed by chemical weapons in all the armies combined.[3] More than one-half of the deaths were Russian soldiers. Many of them may not have had gas masks. It is possible the true number of gas deaths was higher, as some dead were listed as simply killed in action. Many more people were injured by gas, including 185,000 from the United Kingdom and the colonies and other areas it controlled.[4] Most recovered, although a few received disability pensions for their injuries.

BLISTERING POISON

Then an even more horrible gas was introduced in July 1917. Mustard gas caused more casualties than all the other chemical agents combined. Mustard gas worked more slowly but caused large blisters everywhere it touched, inside as well as outside of the body.

Gas masks worked only when people had them and when they recognized a gas attack early. Harry L. Gilchrist, medical director of the US Army Gas Service,

Many victims of chemical warfare were permanently blinded or otherwise maimed.

described the effects of a mustard gas attack: "At first the troops didn't notice the gas and were not uncomfortable, but in the course of an hour or so, there was marked inflammation of their eyes. They vomited, and there was [redness] of the skin. . . . Later there was severe blistering of the skin, especially where the uniform had been contaminated, and by the time the gassed cases reached the casualty clearing station, the men were virtually blind and had to be led about, each man holding on to the man in front with an orderly in the lead."[5]

It was important to treat mustard gas patients as quickly as possible. Bathing with hot water and soap within 30 minutes of exposure could prevent blistering. After that time, bathing could help reduce blistering. The eyes had to be washed as well to prevent damage. Bath trucks were developed with hot water boilers and several fold-down showerheads. Trained medics accompanied these portable shower units. The troops then received clean clothing while their uniforms were decontaminated.

Even with these precautions, on average it took 46 days to recover from mustard gas because of the damage it caused inside the body. Mustard gas caused more severe lung damage than chlorine or phosgene. Shirley Millard, a US nurse, wrote in her diary about the horrors of caring for mustard gas patients: "Gas cases are terrible. They cannot breathe lying down or sitting up. They just struggle for breath but nothing can be done. . . . their lungs are gone . . . literally burnt out."[6]

GAS MASKS

Gas masks provided the best protection against gas attacks. Early options involved covering the face with cloth soaked in urine or cotton pads dipped in baking soda. This did not help much, but later gas masks were better, although they were sometimes awkward and uncomfortable. Soldiers kept their gas masks at hand and practiced putting them on quickly at a signal.

During and after a chemical weapons attack, stretcher bearers had to use gas masks. This made moving and treating wounded soldiers more challenging. The injured men also needed masks. Putting headgear on a wounded soldier could cause more damage.

The animals used for transportation or sending messages during the war were also often killed or injured by chemical gases. Horses were sometimes given gas masks that fit over their muzzles. The Germans had carrier pigeon cases that were protected from gas.

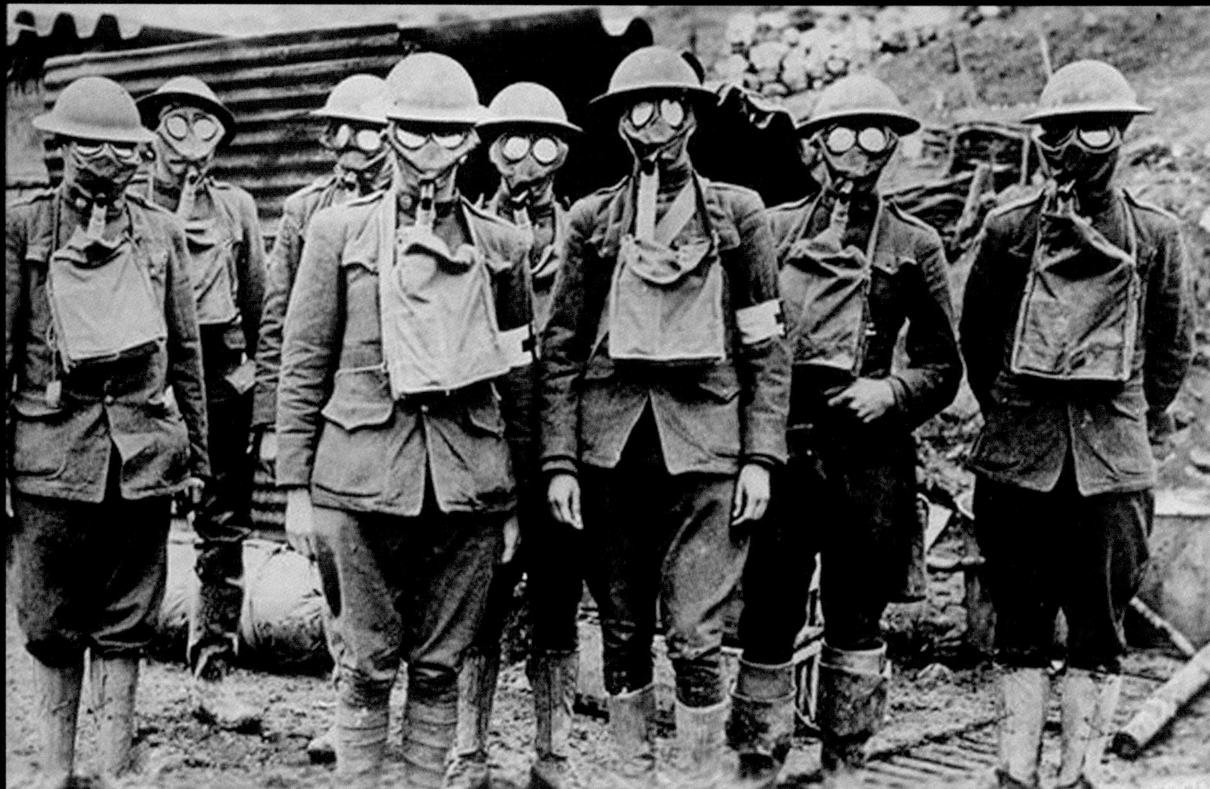

Gas masks protected the head and lungs, but the gas still caused painful blisters on the body.

Medical personnel were in danger as well. A soldier covered in the gas could spread it to the ambulance, other patients, and the medical help. Heavier than air or water, the gas settled in ditches and trenches and caused problems long after an attack. A contaminated area could injure people or animals who disturbed it.

GAS SHOCK

The fear of gas attacks caused mental stress as well. Fear could even cause physical symptoms. After a shell exploded near a group of US Army soldiers while they ate, panic set in. A soldier remembered someone yelling "Gas!" and claiming the food had been gassed. "All the men were seized with gas fright and a few minutes later made their way to the Aid Station. . . . They came in in stooping posture, holding their abdomens and complaining of pains in the stomach, while their faces bore anxious, frightened expressions and some had even vomited."[7] The symptoms came purely from their imaginations.

Panics such as this were common enough doctors had a hard time telling if an attack was real. They generally allowed the men to rest and waited to see if symptoms would appear. If symptoms did not appear, the soldiers were sent back to the trenches. If they had been exposed, the treatment was simple: oxygen and bed rest.

Doctors working at the battlefields did their best to ease the effects of poison gas. At the same time, other doctors were helping develop chemical warfare. Chemists worked with doctors to understand how gases would affect human bodies. Therefore, World War I doctors were instrumental in creating weapons and making them more destructive, as well as fighting the effects of those weapons.

The dazed stare, *lower left*, was one supposed symptom of shell shock.

CHAPTER 8

SHELL SHOCK

Gas shock was only one form of emotional trauma soldiers suffered. For many soldiers, the horrors of war were too great to bear. The stress of fear and constant violence led to a condition known as shell shock. The British army alone dealt with 80,000 cases of shell shock.[1] Some soldiers were unable to eat or had diarrhea. Many developed nervous twitching and uncontrollable shaking. Some developed pain or cramps in the same body regions they had injured in enemy soldiers. Snipers went blind with no physical cause.

Psychological illnesses were not well understood before or during the war. At first, many people believed physical factors caused shell shock. For example, exhaustion, brain damage from nearby explosions, and carbon monoxide poisoning were viewed as possible factors. Or perhaps a physical trauma, such as being buried alive or exposure to heavy bombing, had injured the nerves. If the problem was physical, then it should be treated physically, or so the logic went. Rest, massage, a good diet, and electric shock treatments were recommended and administered.

But men who had never been at the front lines came down with shell shock. Psychoanalyst Ernest Jones blamed the fact that war caused men to go against their ideals. Men were allowed and even ordered to behave in an uncivilized manner. They had to do and see things that went against their morals.

After he was hospitalized for a breakdown, Arthur Hubbard, a British soldier, wrote about one battle: "We had strict orders not to take prisoners, no matter if wounded my first job was when I had finished cutting some of their wire away, to empty my magazine on 3 Germans that came out of one of their

VARYING DIAGNOSES

What diagnosis soldiers received for mental conditions depended partly on their class. A diagnosis might be made on the basis of symptoms, such as paralysis or convulsions. In some countries, these symptoms were often diagnosed as hysteria. This was considered either an inherited family disease or a condition arising out of the patient's personal weakness. In other words, it did not have external causes. The same symptoms could be diagnosed as neurasthenia, which could have external causes. A neurasthenia diagnosis was therefore seen as more honorable. At least in some countries, low-ranking soldiers were more likely to get a diagnosis of hysteria. Officers were more likely to be diagnosed with neurasthenia. Physicians may have had more sympathy for officers because the two groups typically came from the same social class.

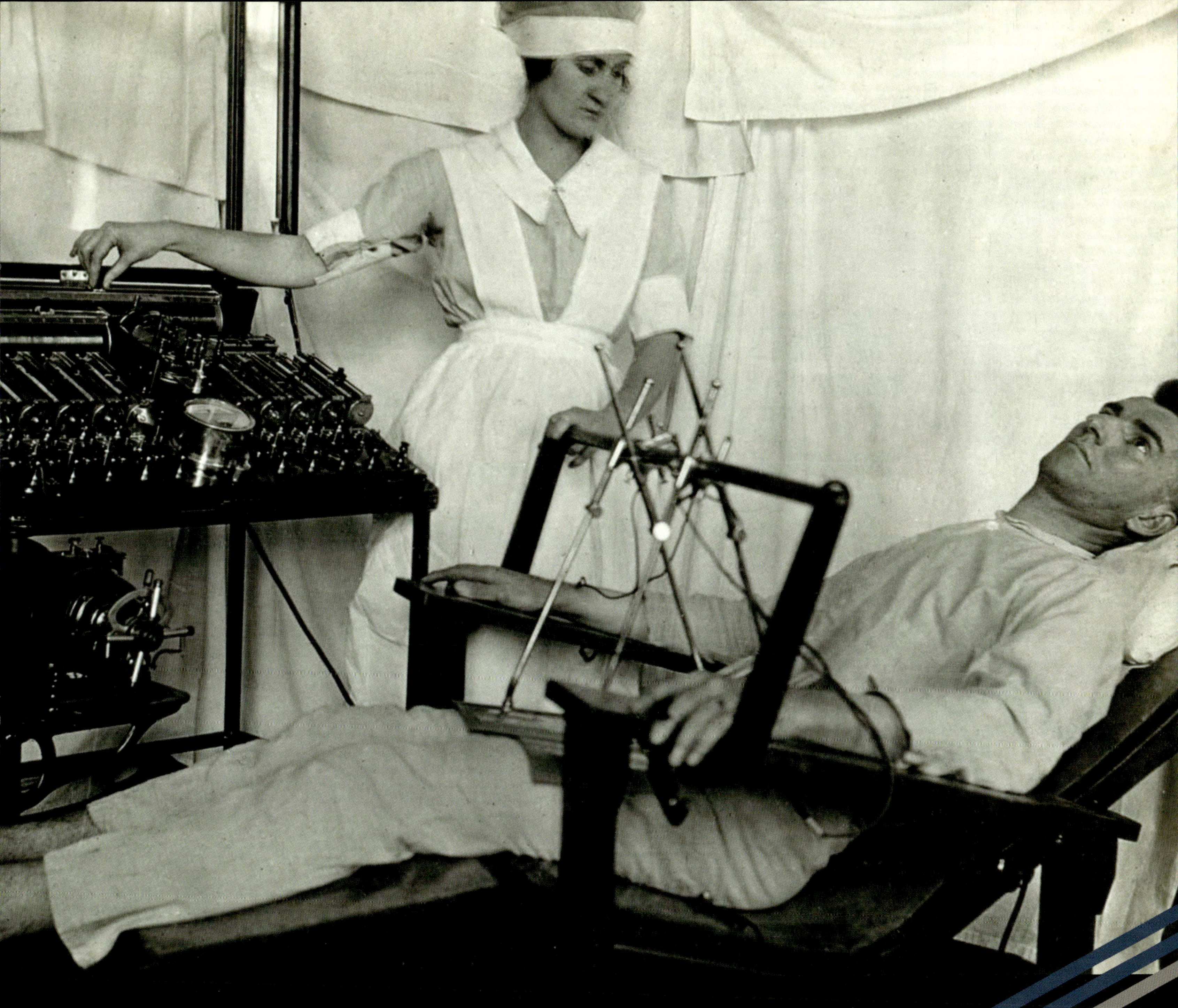

A soldier receives electric shock treatment.

deep dugouts. . . and put them out of misery. They cried for mercy, but I had my orders. . . . It makes my head jump to think about it."[2] Most of his battalion was killed during the ensuing battle. Hubbard was buried and had to dig himself out. He was then almost killed by machine-gun fire during the retreat. Experiences such as this were all too common, and the fear and guilt often caused physical symptoms.

TRAUMATIC NEUROSIS

In Germany, psychologists had explored the idea of traumatic neurosis in the decades before the war. Traumatic neurosis refers to physical symptoms stemming from a traumatic event, such as an accident. Today, this is called post-traumatic stress disorder (PTSD). Symptoms can include anxiety, nightmares, and flashbacks. Patients may have trouble concentrating, remembering, or sleeping. However, some German experts declared the traumatic neurosis theory wrong in 1916. The new prevailing belief was anyone with a mental disorder had to have been sick before the war. War alone was not seen as a cause for psychological suffering. Rather, the war might have exposed a previous illness. This debate went on in many countries. PTSD would not be widely understood and accepted as a diagnosis until decades later.

In every country, people who had not experienced the trauma of battle for themselves often had a hard time believing in this invisible injury. Many doctors and officials saw shell shock as a sign of weakness or a way to avoid going back to battle. Government officials also had a practical reason to deny the existence of shell shock. Wounded soldiers could get pensions, and that cost their country money. The war was expensive enough, so giving too many pensions was discouraged. At first, British soldiers could get a diagnosis of either shell shock wounded or shell shock sick. The former meant the shell shock was due to enemy action, and the diagnosis would allow the patient a pension. If the breakdown did not immediately follow a shell explosion, it was considered a sickness rather than a wound, and the patient could not get a pension. Later, British doctors avoided the term *shell shock* altogether, instead using Not yet Diagnosed (Nervous). At the end of the war, they were forbidden from identifying a patient as shell shock wounded. The decision was financial, not medical.

RECEIVING PENSIONS

Two years after the war's end, almost 65,000 men were receiving pensions for shell shock from the British army alone.[3] These government payments helped support soldiers who were too injured or sick to work. Some soldiers may have exaggerated their suffering to avoid being sent back to the front, or to continue receiving benefits. However, it is now thought most shell shock victims were truly ill.

SEARCHING FOR A CURE

Some base hospitals specialized in psychiatric disorders, but doctors did not have reliable cures for shell shock. They also had pressure to cure the sick quickly to

Shell shock patients in a psychiatric ward in Allerey, France

get them back to the fighting. If patients could not be made fit for battle, they could at least be sent to the arms factories that made weapons, where they would be useful and not a drain on the system. That meant a focus on getting rid of the symptoms instead of helping the patient emotionally.

Most military psychiatric hospitals were designed to resemble barracks so the sick would not see their treatment as a break from the war. Treatments varied but were typically forceful and even harsh. Electric treatments could be very painful and sometimes led to charges of abuse.

Psychoanalysis was a fairly new field and not well accepted during the war. Psychoanalysts saw the opportunity to promote their treatment style, which they believed was more humane. Their method involved hypnosis and discussion sessions with a therapist.

Regardless of the treatment, shell shock patients received little sympathy. Their disorder was viewed as shameful and weak. The treatment of shell shock could be seen as one of the medical failures of World War I. However, the large number of patients, and the controversies surrounding their treatment, had some long-term benefits. The situation contributed to a better understanding of psychological trauma. By World War II, psychological issues were better understood.

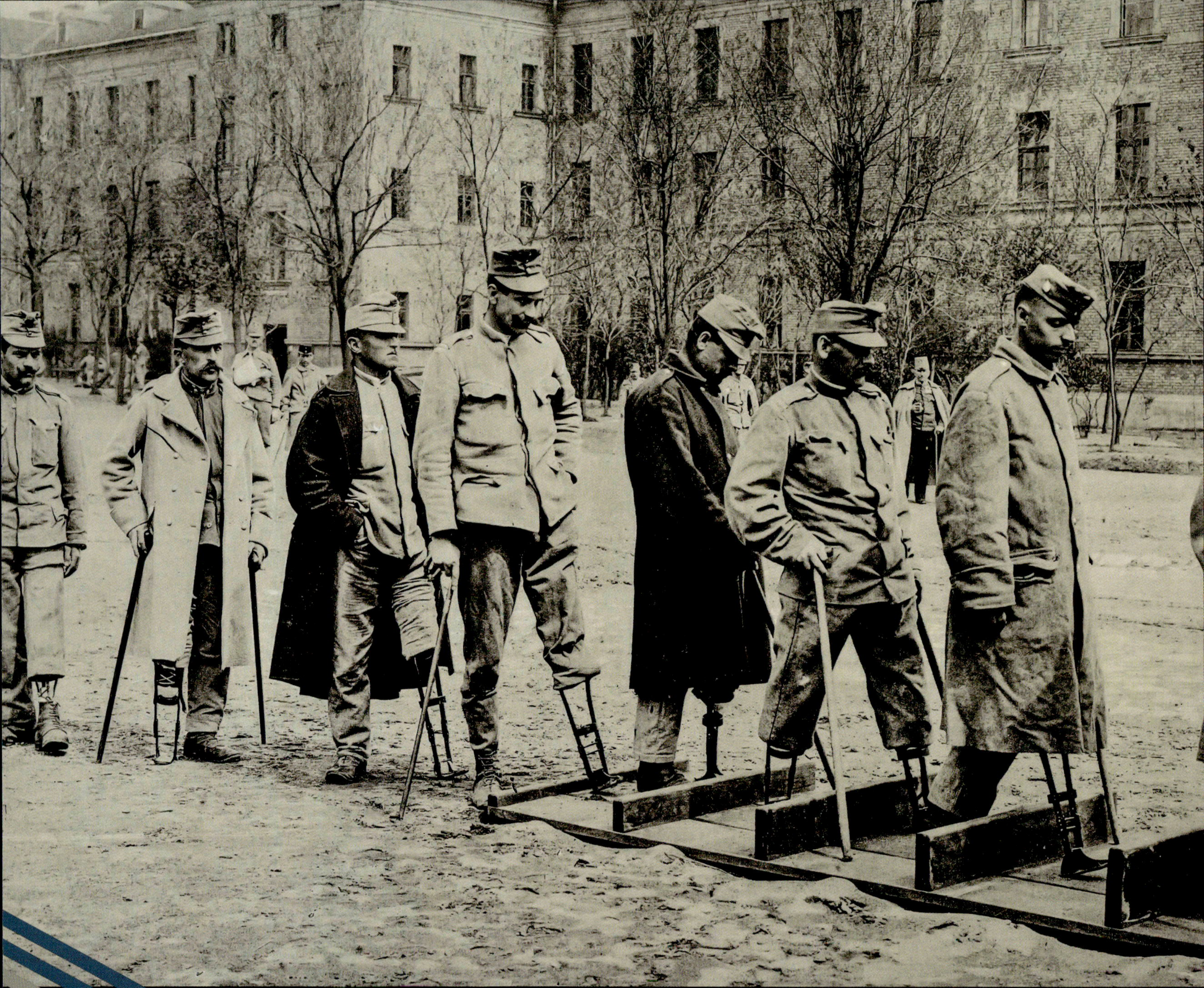

After returning home, soldiers from Hungary learn to walk on their new artificial legs.

CHAPTER 9

CONTINUING CARE

The fighting ended after the Allies and Germany signed an armistice, or temporary truce, that went into effect on November 11, 1918. Yet the effects of the war would be felt for many years, especially among veterans and the medical community.

After the war ended, it took months to get all the medical personnel home. Many wounded soldiers still needed care. The Spanish Flu also created new waves of patients. In addition, arranging transportation took time. For the Americans serving in Europe, not enough transport ships existed to carry everyone at once. Most units did not make it home until 1919.

With the end of the fighting, doctors' priorities were no longer getting soldiers back to the battle. However, they still faced pressure to keep wounded soldiers from being a drain on their nations' governments. If too many soldiers could not work and therefore had to receive government pensions, the nation could go bankrupt. Soldiers who received therapy or prosthetic limbs might be able to return to work. That was good for the government as well as the individual.

Attitudes toward soldiers receiving pensions varied somewhat by country. In the United Kingdom, an injured soldier had to prove his injury was war related to receive a pension. In most countries, people believed the government had some responsibility to care for injured soldiers not only during the war but afterward.

After the war, the idea of an individual's right to long-term medical care spread to the broader community in some countries but not all of them. Some soldiers were not able to work after the war, but doctors could make their lives easier. Doctors, and society at large, generally had more sympathy for obvious physical injuries, such as missing limbs, than for invisible mental illnesses. Even physical diseases that did not show outwardly, such as lung problems, received less sympathy than noticeable ones.

Long-term medical care varied by country, and sometimes by the race or religion of the patient. For example, more than 14,000 wounded Indian soldiers and officers were brought to England for treatment.[1] In general, British hospitals tried to accommodate the special needs of Indian patients. British officials did not want to risk offending Indians and perhaps setting off a rebellion in the Indian colony. Therefore, patients were often segregated by religion and served by orderlies of the same religion. Separate areas were set aside for prayers by Muslims, Hindus, and Sikhs.

Indian patients were largely kept separate from the local English people. Officials wanted to ensure the Indians kept respect for their British rulers. Many officials feared too much mingling would lead to disrespect. Some hospitals allowed outings in supervised small groups. But at others, restrictions and discipline were harsh, hurting patient morale. At the Kitchener Indian Hospital in Brighton, barbed wire and police guards turned the hospital into a prison for the patients. No women nurses were allowed to work at Kitchener, for fear they might mix with the Indian patients and cause a

Soldiers with artificial limbs were taught how to make use of their new appendages.

WOODEN LEG FOR A HEROIC BIRD

Humans were not the only ones who lost limbs during the war. Carrier pigeons were used by both sides to carry messages during World War I. Perhaps the most famous World War I carrier pigeon was Cher Ami, French for "Dear Friend." A US Army major whose troops were surrounded by Germans released Cher Ami with a message. German soldiers fired on the pigeon and Cher Ami fell. But the bird got up and flew 25 miles (40 km) despite serious injuries. Cher Ami is credited with saving more than 200 lives. Medics saved the bird's life and carved him a tiny wooden leg to replace the one he lost.

scandal. Rules were relaxed somewhat later during the war, after the strict policies set off protests.

RETURNING TO THE WORKFORCE

Soldiers with missing limbs were seen as heroic. It was assumed they had fought bravely, and missing limbs were signs of their valor and sacrifice. At specialist centers, soldiers with lost limbs were fitted with new limbs and taught how to use them. At Queen Mary's Hospital in Roehampton, England, which opened to patients on July 16, 1917, patients were also encouraged to "Learn a Trade!" As they recovered from their injuries, patients were sometimes taught skills that would help them find work after the war. These activities included carpentry, engineering, bookkeeping, poultry farming, toy making, dentistry, hairdressing, clock repair, and cinema operation. Patients even worked in hospital workshops making artificial limbs.

Many newspapers printed articles about wounded soldiers learning to live—and even run, bicycle, and box—with their artificial limbs. Returning to work was viewed as important for several reasons. It allowed a soldier to become a productive member of society again. It also allowed him to fulfill traditional ideas of masculinity. An article on the hospital declared, "They come to Roehampton in thousands, disabled, crippled men. They leave, redeemed by human skill; no longer useless, limbless creatures, but men anxious and fit to work again and take a place in the world of workers."[2]

FACING THE MIRROR

In some ways, injured soldiers with lost limbs were luckier than those who suffered facial injuries. Thousands of soldiers suffered damage to the face from wounds or burns. Some facial injuries interfered with normal activities, such as eating. Maxillofacial surgery treats problems in the head and neck. It was adapted from dental surgery techniques used to repair damaged jaws.

But repairing function was not enough to return an injured soldier to normal life. Soldiers with damaged faces often shocked or frightened people, so the soldiers believed they had to cover up their faces or avoid going out in public. During the war, they were not sent back to battle, even if they were capable of fighting. It was believed seeing them would destroy morale. After the war, severe facial injuries were enough to provide a man with a pension. The shame and loss of identity were viewed as a serious disability, even for a man otherwise able to work.

Reconstructive surgery, designed to improve a patient's appearance after an illness or injury, has been practiced for centuries. Beginning in the 1800s, the term *plastic surgery* was sometimes used. World War I encouraged many advances in this field.

SHOCK AND DESPAIR

Doctors and nurses had to hide their reactions to disfigured faces. The sight of a damaged face was a shock to no one more than the injured soldier. Mirrors were banned in most hospital wards. Men who caught a glimpse of their own reflection sometimes collapsed in shock. US surgeon Dr. Fred Albee wrote, "The psychological effect on a man who must go through life, an object of horror to himself as well as to others, is beyond description. . . . It must be unmitigated hell to feel like a stranger to yourself."[3]

Sometimes relatively simple techniques were enough. Skin grafting, in which fresh skin is placed over a damaged area, was already known. Russia and Germany had made advances in this area before the war. But many World War I soldiers suffered from much more serious disfiguration. Surgeons had to learn on the job. Some surgeons tried to reconstruct the soldiers' faces so they would feel comfortable going out in society. Surgeon Harold Gillies worked with Charles Auguste Valadier, a dental specialist, to rebuild faces. Artists created sculptures to show what the men had looked like before their injuries, and surgeons attempted to recreate the original face with prosthetic faces, noses, and face masks.

HAROLD GILLIES

1882–1960

Surgeon Harold Gillies was born in New Zealand and studied at the University of Cambridge in England. During World War I, he served in field ambulances in France and Belgium. He saw the terrible damage done to the faces of soldiers fighting in the trenches. He also met Hippolyte Morestin, a famous French surgeon who specialized in face and jaw injuries. Gillies decided to specialize in facial reconstruction.

He saw the need for a special care unit and convinced the United Kingdom to set up such a unit. Gillies commanded the unit, which served approximately 11,000 patients during the war. After the war, he continued his work in reconstructive surgery and made several important innovations. He saw the need for a dental surgeon to be on hand during a face operation. He encouraged anesthetists to develop new techniques for giving patients anesthesia, because a face mask did not work during facial surgery. During World War II, Gillies headed a team to provide plastic surgery for soldiers. He was knighted in the United Kingdom and received honors from the Danish and Norwegian governments for his work and contributions.

The advances in reconstructive surgery developed during and after World War I helped treat the casualties of World War II. Yet even today, modern techniques would struggle to treat the severe facial injuries from World War I.

In the United Kingdom alone, an estimated 6,500 soldiers received head or eye injuries.[4] Not all of these patients needed a complete mask. Dark glasses could cover up a damaged eye, or a prosthetic nose could replace a missing one. At most, a few thousand masks were made.

GOING HOME

Despite the often horrific conditions of the war, many doctors and nurses were sad to go home. They believed they would

A French soldier wears a sculpted and painted face mask to cover injuries on his lower face.

miss the challenging cases and especially the teams they had grown so close to while working together.

Claims have been made that wars are good for medicine, because of the advances that happen during wartime. However, every period has its advances. During World War I, some fields of medicine did advance dramatically, such as the treatment of shock. A few advances, such as the treatment of diseases brought on by trench warfare, lost importance after the war. Whether war is good for medicine is debatable. But certainly, medicine is good for war.

NEW FACES

US physician and American Red Cross director Maynard Ladd founded the Studio for Portrait Masks. His wife, Anna Coleman Watts Ladd, a sculptor, worked with four assistants. They took up to a month to make one mask, first making a plaster cast of the patient's face. This would be used, perhaps along with a photograph, to build a portrait out of clay. A mask was then made from very thin galvanized copper and painted to resemble skin. The masks did not change expression, and they did not help the patient with actions such as chewing or swallowing. But they did allow the soldiers to show their faces with more confidence.

TIMELINE

June 28, 1914

Gavrilo Princip assassinates Austria-Hungary's Archduke Franz Ferdinand.

July 28, 1914

Austria declares war on Serbia.

October 1914

Marie Curie outfits her first radiology van, providing X-ray machines to wounded soldiers at the battlefront.

November 1914

Typhus fever kills many thousands of soldiers, civilians, and prisoners of war.

May 1916

The British army receives a mobile dental laboratory, the start of improving dental care.

1917

US Army doctor Captain Oswald Robertson establishes the first blood bank on the western front.

April 6, 1917

The United States declares war on Germany, officially entering the war.

July 1917

Mustard gas joins the arsenal of chemical weaponry.

Winter 1914

The first cases of trench foot appear.

April 22, 1915

German chlorine gas kills more than 1,000 French and Algerian soldiers and wounds another 4,000.

1916

Britain introduces a draft, but doctors are exempt so they can tend to health care at home.

1916

Alexis Carrel and Henry Drysdale Dakin develop the Carrel–Dakin solution to clean wounds.

July 16, 1917

Queen Mary's Hospital in Roehampton, England, opens to patients.

March 11, 1918

The first US case of what will be called Spanish Flu hits a military camp in Kansas.

1918

By the end of the year, millions have died worldwide from Spanish Flu.

November 11, 1918

Germany signs an armistice with the Allies, officially ending the war.

ESSENTIAL FACTS

KEY PLAYERS

- US Army doctor Captain Oswald Robertson established the first blood bank on the western front in 1917. He used sodium citrate, a salt, to keep the blood from coagulating.
- British surgeon Harold Gillies worked with a dental specialist, Charles Auguste Valadier, to rebuild faces injured in battle.
- Polish-born physicist Marie Curie convinced the French government to let her set up military radiology centers. By late October 1914, she outfitted the first traveling radiology van. Eventually 20 radiology vans provided X-ray machines to the wounded at the battlefront.

KEY DATES

- April 22, 1915: The world entered a new phase of chemical warfare as German forces released chlorine gas against French forces at Ypres, Belgium.
- 1916: Alexis Carrel and Henry Drysdale Dakin developed the Carrel-Dakin solution, an antiseptic that was used to flush and successfully treat wounds.
- March 11, 1918: More than 100 soldiers at Fort Riley, Kansas, came down with cold-like symptoms. The disease traveled to Europe with US soldiers heading to the battlefields and quickly spread.

IMPACT ON SOCIETY

- Medical personnel developed a better understanding of how to treat shock. Advances in blood transfusions, including the ability to store blood, improved the process.
- Advances in wound treatment led to a better understanding of infections. This encouraged more hygienic practices and better future treatments. Antiseptic solutions developed during the war not only saved lives but also allowed more injured soldiers to keep their limbs.
- Doctors could do little for flu or pneumonia patients, but tracking disease helped researchers understand how diseases spread.
- Although treatments of psychological diseases were poor, the large number of patients contributed to a better understanding of psychological trauma. By World War II, psychological issues would be better understood.
- Advances were made in physical therapy and reconstructive surgery.

QUOTE

"We soon learnt to give up no case as hopeless."

– *Henry Souttar*

GLOSSARY

ANESTHETIC
A substance that causes a loss of consciousness or an insensitivity to pain; used to reduce suffering during surgical procedures.

ANTISEPTIC
A preparation that cleans and disinfects to prevent the growth of disease-causing germs.

ARMISTICE
A temporary stop of fighting by mutual agreement.

ARTILLERY
Large guns manned by a crew of operators used to shoot long distances.

CIVILIAN
A person not serving in the armed forces.

DRAFT
A system in which people of a certain age are required to register for military service.

FRONT
An area where a battle is taking place.

INTRAVENOUSLY
Through or within a vein.

NO-MAN'S-LAND
The dangerous territory lying between opposing trenches targeted by artillery and snipers and lined with barbed wire obstructions to slow enemy advances.

PATHOLOGIST
A doctor who studies the way disease changes the body and examines bodies to discover the cause of death.

PENSION
A regular payment made to a retired person as a reward for past services, or to help someone suffering from an injury or other need.

PROPAGANDA
Information used to support a political group or point of view, or to persuade the audience to support their country's participation in a war.

SHRAPNEL
Shell fragments from an exploded shell.

TRANSFUSION
The act of transferring blood or similar products from one person or animal to another.

ADDITIONAL RESOURCES

SELECTED BIBLIOGRAPHY

Greenwood, John T. and F. Clifton Berry. *Medics at War: Military Medicine from Colonial Times to the 21st Century*. Naval Institute, 2005. Print.

Souttar, Henry Sessions. "A Surgeon in Belgium." *Project Gutenberg*. Project Gutenberg, n.d. Web. 15 May 2015.

Stephen Western. "The Royal Army Medical Corps and the Role of the Field Ambulance on the Western Front, 1914–1918." *University of Birmingham*. University of Birmingham, Sept. 2011. Web. 2 Apr. 2015.

FURTHER READINGS

Adams, Simon. *DK World War I*. New York: DK Publishing, 2014. Print.

Freedman, Russell. *The War to End All Wars: World War I*. Boston: Clarion Books, 2010. Print.

Grant, R. G. *World War I: The Definitive Visual History: From Sarajevo to Versailles*. New York: DK Publishing, 2014. Print.

WEBSITES

To learn more about Essential Library of World War I, visit **booklinks.abdopublishing.com.** These links are routinely monitored and updated to provide the most current information available.

PLACES TO VISIT

National Archives
700 Pennsylvania Avenue NW
Washington, DC 20408
866-272-6272
http://www.archives.gov
Records from World War I are available online and at the archives.

National World War I Museum
100 W. Twenty-Sixth Street
Kansas City, MO 64108
816-888-8100
https://theworldwar.org
Exhibits and educational programs explore the history of World War I and share stories through the eyes of those who lived it. The museum is attached to the Liberty Memorial, a monument to those who served.

SOURCE NOTES

CHAPTER 1. IN THE MIDST OF BATTLE

1. "World War I." *HistoryNet*. World History Group, 2015. Web. 6 Apr. 2015.

2. Christine M. Kreiserand. "Battlefield Medics: Saving Lives Under Fire." *HistoryNet*. World History Group, 12 June 2006. Web. 6 Apr. 2015.

3. Leo van Bergen. "Medicine and Medical Service." *1914–1918 Online: International Encyclopedia of the First World War*. 1914–1918 Online: International Encyclopedia of the First World War, 30 June 2015. Web. 1 July 2015.

4. Henry Sessions Souttar. "A Surgeon in Belgium." *Project Gutenberg*. Project Gutenberg, 14 Feb. 2004. Web. 1 Apr. 2015.

5. Stephen Western. "The Royal Army Medical Corps and the Role of the Field Ambulance on the Western Front, 1914–1918." *University of Birmingham*. University of Birmingham, Sept. 2011. Web. 2 Apr. 2015.

6. Henry Sessions Souttar. "A Surgeon in Belgium." *Project Gutenberg*. Project Gutenberg, 14 Feb. 2004. Web. 1 Apr. 2015.

CHAPTER 2. GETTING HELP FAST

1. "Casualties in France." *Doctor Brighton's Pavilion*. SikhMuseum.com, 2012. Web. 27 May 2015.

2. "Trauma Resuscitation." *Trauma.org*. Trauma.org, n.d. Web. 6 Apr. 2015.

3. Henry Sessions Souttar. "A Surgeon in Belgium." *Project Gutenberg*. Project Gutenberg, 14 Feb. 2004. Web. 1 Apr. 2015.

4. Ibid.

5. Kirsty Harris. "Red Reflections on the Sea: Australian Army Nurses Serving at Sea in World War 1." *Academia*. Academia, 2015. Web. 4 Apr. 2015.

6. Henry Sessions Souttar. "A Surgeon in Belgium." *Project Gutenberg*. Project Gutenberg, 14 Feb. 2004. Web. 1 Apr. 2015.

7. Christine M. Kreiserand. "Battlefield Medics: Saving Lives Under Fire." *HistoryNet*. World History Group, 12 June 2006. Web. 6 Apr. 2015.

8. Henry Sessions Souttar. "A Surgeon in Belgium." *Project Gutenberg*. Project Gutenberg, 14 Feb. 2004. Web. 1 Apr. 2015.

9. Leo van Bergen. "Medicine and Medical Service." *1914–1918 Online: International Encyclopedia of the First World War*. 1914–1918 Online: International Encyclopedia of the First World War, 30 June 2015. Web. 1 July 2015.

10. Ibid.

11. Stephen Western. "The Royal Army Medical Corps and the Role of the Field Ambulance on the Western Front, 1914–1918." *University of Birmingham*. University of Birmingham, Sept. 2011. Web. 2 Apr. 2015.

12. "RAVC History." *Army Medical Services Museum*. Army Medical Services Museum, n.d. Web. 4 Apr. 2015.

13. "Our History." *American Red Cross*. The American National Red Cross, 2015. Web. 14 Apr. 2015.

CHAPTER 3. ADVANCES IN SURGERY

1. Owain Clarke. "World War One: Medical Advances Inspired by the Conflict." *BBC News*. BBC, 7 Aug. 2014. Web. 3 Apr. 2015.

2. Leo van Bergen. "Medicine and Medical Service." *1914–1918 Online: International Encyclopedia of the First World War*. 1914–1918 Online: International Encyclopedia of the First World War, 30 June 2015. Web. 1 July 2015.

3. Henry Sessions Souttar. "A Surgeon in Belgium." *Project Gutenberg*. Project Gutenberg, 14 Feb. 2004. Web. 1 Apr. 2015.

CHAPTER 4. WARDING OFF INFECTION

1. Surgeon-General Sir Anthony Bowlby. "The Bradshaw Lecture on Wounds in War." *The Britain Medical Journal*. The Britain Medical Journal, 25 Dec. 1915. Web. 8 Apr. 2015.

2. "Losing a Limb on the Battlefield." *Brought to Life: Exploring the History of Medicine*. Science Museum, n.d. Web. 5 Apr. 2015.

3. Dr. Howard Markel. "The Real Story behind Penicillin." *PBS NewsHour*. NewsHour Productions, 27 Sept. 2013. Web. 8 Apr. 2015.

4. "Military Nurses in World War I." *History and Collections*. Women in Military Service for America Memorial Foundation, n.d. Web. 6 Apr. 2015.

5. Ibid.

6. Kirsty Harris. "Red Reflections on the Sea: Australian Army Nurses Serving at Sea in World War 1." *Academia*. Academia, 2015. Web. 4 Apr. 2015.

7. Ibid.

8. Ibid.

9. Ibid.

SOURCE NOTES CONTINUED

CHAPTER 5. THE WAR AGAINST DISEASE

1. Francis Cox. "The First World War: Disease, the Only Victor." *Gresham College*. Gresham College, Mar. 2014. Web. 13 Apr. 2015.

2. David W. Tschanz. "Typhus Fever on the Eastern Front in World War I." *Montana State University Entomology Group*. Montana State University Entomology Group, n.d. Web. 17 Apr. 2015.

3. Carol R. Byerly. "The U.S. Military and the Influenza Pandemic of 1918–1919." *Public Health Reports*. National Center for Biotechnology Information, 2010. Web. 13 Apr. 2015.

4. "Roses of No Man's Land: Casualties & Illness." *Wisconsin Veterans Museum*. Wisconsin Veterans Museum, 2011. Web. 13 Apr. 2015.

5. Christine M. Kreiserand. "Battlefield Medics: Saving Lives Under Fire." *HistoryNet*. World History Group, 12 June 2006. Web. 6 Apr. 2015.

6. Richard Marshall. "The British Army's Fight against Venereal Disease in the 'Heroic Age of Prostitution.'" *World War I Centenary*. University of Oxford, n.d. Web. 14 Apr. 2015.

7. Carol R. Byerly. "The U.S. Military and the Influenza Pandemic of 1918–1919." *Public Health Reports*. National Center for Biotechnology Information, 2010. Web. 13 Apr. 2015.

8. Francis Cox. "The First World War: Disease, the Only Victor." *Gresham College*. Gresham College, Mar. 2014. Web. 13 Apr. 2015.

9. "Influenza Pandemics." *The History of Vaccines*. The College of Physicians of Philadelphia, 2015. Web. 14. Apr. 2015.

CHAPTER 6. TRENCH WARFARE

1. Frederick Holmes. "Trench Fever in the First World War." *KU Medical Center*. The University of Kansas Medical Center, 2015. Web. 9 Apr. 2015.

2. "Casualties in France." *Doctor Brighton's Pavilion*. SikhMuseum.com, 2012. Web. 27 May 2015.

3. Kirsty Harris. "Red Reflections on the Sea: Australian Army Nurses Serving at Sea in World War 1." *Academia*. Academia, 2015. Web. 4 Apr. 2015.

CHAPTER 7. THE CHEMISTS' WAR

1. Gerard J. Fitzgerald. "Chemical Warfare and Medical Response During World War I." *American Public Health Association.* National Center for Biotechnology Information, Apr. 2008. Web. 15 Apr. 2015.

2. Ibid.

3. Marek Pruszewicz. "How Deadly Was the Poison Gas of WW1?" *BBC News.* BBC, 30 Jan. 2015. Web. 15 Apr. 2015.

4. Ibid.

5. Gerard J. Fitzgerald. "Chemical Warfare and Medical Response During World War I." *American Public Health Association.* National Center for Biotechnology Information, Apr. 2008. Web. 15 Apr. 2015.

6. Shirley Millard. *I Saw Them Die: Diary and Recollections of Shirley Millard.* New Orleans: Quid Pro, 2011. Print.

7. Gerard J. Fitzgerald. "Chemical Warfare and Medical Response During World War I." *American Public Health Association.* National Center for Biotechnology Information, Apr. 2008. Web. 15 Apr. 2015.

CHAPTER 8. SHELL SHOCK

1. Joanna Bourke. "Shell Shock during World War One." *BBC.* BBC, 10 Mar. 2011. Web. 16 Apr. 2015.

2. Leo van Bergen. "Medicine and Medical Service." *1914–1918 Online: International Encyclopedia of the First World War.* 1914–1918 Online: International Encyclopedia of the First World War, 30 June 2015. Web. 1 July 2015.

3. "Myofascial Pain Management." *Pain Education.* Dr. Simon L. Strauss, 2015. Web. 7 Apr. 2015.

CHAPTER 9. CONTINUING CARE

1. "Casualties in France." *Doctor Brighton's Pavilion.* SikhMuseum.com, 2012. Web. 27 May 2015.

2. Suzannah Biernoff. "The Rhetoric of Disfigurement in First World War Britain." *Social History of Medicine.* National Center for Biotechnology Information, Dec. 2011. Web. 16 Apr. 2015.

3. Ibid.

4. Ibid.

INDEX

ABOUT THE AUTHOR

Chris Eboch, aka M. M. Eboch, writes about science, history, and culture for all ages. Her recent nonfiction titles include *Chaco Canyon*, *Living with Dyslexia*, and *The Green Movement*. Her novels for young people include *The Genie's Gift*, a Middle Eastern fantasy; *The Eyes of Pharaoh*, a mystery in ancient Egypt; *The Well of Sacrifice*, a Mayan adventure; and the Haunted series, which starts with *The Ghost on the Stairs*.